GLOBAL JOBS

FOR

History Majors

Stephen Lambert and Julie DeGalan

McGraw Hill

New York Chicago San Francisco Lisbon London Madrid Mexico City
Milan New Delhi San Juan Seoul Singapore Sydney Toronto

Library of Congress Cataloging-in-Publication Data

Lambert, Stephen E.
    Great jobs for history majors / by Stephen Lambert and Julie DeGalan. — 3rd ed.
       p.   cm.
    DeGalan's name appears first on the earlier edition.
    Includes index.
    ISBN 0-07-148213-X (alk. paper)
    1. History—Vocational guidance. 2. College graduates—Employment. I. DeGalan, Julie. II. Title.

D16.9.D34 2007
650.14—dc22
                                                      2007010793

1 2 3 4 5 6 7 8 9 10 11 12 13 14 15 16 17 18 19 20 21 22   DOC/DOC   0 9 8 7

ISBN 978-0-07-148213-4
MHID   0-07-148213-X

McGraw-Hill books are available at special quantity discounts to use as premiums and sales promotions, or for use in corporate training programs. For more information, please write to the Director of Special Sales, Professional Publishing, McGraw-Hill, Two Penn Plaza, New York, NY 10121-2298. Or contact your local bookstore.

This book is printed on acid-free paper.

To Amy Caroline, Matt III, Cynthia, Michael, Constance, and Catherine with all our love.

Contents

Acknowledgments

Special thanks go to Kanako Takei for her assistance in locating useful websites and Tamara Pederson, who provided special insight into how to use historical events to inform the present. The authors also wish to thank Mark Rowh for his assistance in preparing this revision.

Introduction

"History: The memory of things said and done." —Carl Becker

Carl Becker's definition of history is wonderful because it reminds us that history is the recollection of humanity or what particular people have recalled about other people. Those recollections, or memories, are influenced by the "rememberers" themselves and the influences and biases of their own lives. Just as the word *memory* conjures up an idea of something not quite substantial, not entirely reliable, and subject to verification, we need to remember that history is more memory than fact.

Because what are the facts? Some would say there is no such thing. Each event in life recorded as history is subtly altered by the recorder. That individual, try as he or she might to be objective, alters the record of the event for all time by filtering it through his or her own mind, with individual impressions, perceptions, biases, and judgments. The historian's choice of words, selection of topics and features, emphases, and omissions ultimately constitute the "facts."

Most important for the history major to affirm is the emphasis in this quotation on humanity, because humanity is the stuff of history's people and their legacies. Both the participants in the events and the recorders of those events alike are part of the endless stream of humanity, which is the essential subject of history. And, as with anything human, including dreams, it is subject to interpretation.

Making sense of this record of humanity begins by truly understanding events, analyzing and appreciating what has taken place. Documenting the facts may mean collecting the facts from a number of different observers of the same event. The formal court records of King Henry V, the letters home from a visiting delegation of French ministers, and the diary of a lady-in-waiting may all tell very different versions of the same story. The differences are due to perspective.

For the historian, the history student, or the history graduate consider-ing any of the careers in this book, the greatest gift of the study of history may be the development of a sense of perspective. Perspective is the rare abil-ity to place people, events, and artifacts in true relation to their setting and to assign them a sense of their relative importance. Whether it be assessing a statue of Churchill or Madonna, a Ming vase or the early McDonald's road-side architecture, or a new business acquisition or a product quality lawsuit, the history major who has learned perspective in his or her academic stud-ies has earned a lifelong and career-valuable skill.

Truly understanding events and the people who populate them, analyz-ing the facts, and appreciating fully what has taken place require an ability to synthesize large amounts of information and draw conclusions based. For example, a study of court cases at the turn of the previous century in a small Southern town, with a population that is overwhelmingly African American, shows that over 90 percent of the court cases involved whites. Obviously this study could make the beginning of a strong argument that African Ameri-cans were not being afforded due legal process in that town at that time.

The ability to understand events, analyze and appreciate what has taken place, and then synthesize the resulting information to draw conclusions is essential to the historian and a valuable skill learned in the study of history with broad application. These abilities are then combined with a sense of sequence and a natural curiosity to do the necessary detective work. Because when only pieces of evidence appear, extrapolations must be done relying on others' evidence or listening and reading others' accounts and judiciously assessing the information provided.

Hypotheses are drawn, but they are only as strong as the care and qual-ity of the information that has led to them. If you were to listen today to the presentation of a skilled historical interpreter at Salem, Massachusetts, discussing the infamous witch trials and compare that to the presentation twenty years ago, you would find today's explanation far more tentative. We know more now about group psychology and "groupthink." Through the work of women historians such as Laurel Ulrich, we have a new apprecia-tion for the role of women as midwives in colonial America and the enmity that role earned them from men in the community who disapproved of the silent power such life-giving skill gave them. The interpretation of the mur-ders of these women and children has become more psychological, more polit-ical, and more human.

An appropriate metaphor for the historian might be that of the miner, sifting through the mother lode of human events for the nuggets of significance—the events, people, and juxtaposition of conditions that affect humankind. Sifting through much that is undistinguished, the miner comes to appreciate what is truly worthy of his or her effort.

But the "nugget" of history is not yet ready to be delivered forth to the public. It needs to be assayed for purity, for its value. The miner may then sand or polish this nugget so we can all truly appreciate its worth and importance, giving it a setting that allows us to value its meaning in our lives. Historical facts are like this. They are discovered amid the loose material of past civilizations, and it is the historian's role to appreciate and perceive their importance to history. Before exclaiming "Eureka!" the historian/miner must test the value of the find by assessment. Collaboration, other accounts, and independent verification all help to determine the significance of a historical fact.

To help us appreciate this bit of history, the historian needs to put it in perspective—to set the jewel in a mount, as it were. For any event, personage, or discovery, we need to understand the time, culture, attitudes, and opinions of those involved and their relationship to what is happening to them. Because history is humanity, almost every detail of history needs to be placed in its cultural context to have any impact.

Understanding the cultural context of history means the historian must often physically confront evidence, visit sites, and simply be impressed by the silent testimony of documents and artifacts that define history. Later in this book, you will read of the controversy surrounding the use of Internet databases for historical research. Much of that controversy involves the reliability and accuracy of the documents that are transcribed.

To become engaged in an understanding of the physical remains of culture and what they express is essential. Imbued with stories of these cultural artifacts, the historian's understanding is deepened. This enriched understanding of history is essential before the historian can begin to make the kinds of generalizations about the past that are the hallmark of the wise. Art, music, literature, sculpture, clothing, decoration and motifs, the performing arts, design, crafts, and menu offerings are all indicators of what is important to a culture and help create the context that allows the historian to understand humanity and the memories of that humanity in context.

Laurel Ulrich, the Pulitzer Prize–winning historian from Harvard University, progressed in her research from midwifery to an examination of the "ordinary" fabrics of early-American life—dishcloths, table coverings, muslin, plain fabrics—and what they reveal about the role of women in society at that time and the opportunities they had to impact the lives of those around them.

This ability of the historian to make generalizations is the result of years of study, deep reflection, and uncompromising loyalty to what is accurate and verifiable. They are the statements of true wisdom and, as such, are made carefully and respectfully, always fully aware of what remains unknown and undiscovered that can alter the truth as we understand it. But isn't this what history demands of us, whether we practice it in the boardroom or in the re-creation of a colonial plantation? History asks the historian to connect one fact to another.

We see a bed and all its coverlets on display in an early-American living room, and we might incorrectly assume it is located there for the warmth and comfort of the great cooking fireplace. In fact, there was no more sumptuous display of wealth and/or craftsmanship than in the embroidered bed curtains, tatted sheets, and woven coverlets in an early-American home than the master's bed. It conveyed status and displayed the needlework skills of his wife, the valuable articles that had come by ship, and perhaps some oriental carpets from the East. So, for the historian, this bed is a repository of social systems, commerce, trade, geographical knowledge, design and art, and industry.

The "why" of studying history is clear in Carl Becker's quote. We study a story, not to exhume the past and make a religion of what has gone before but—if our intentions are among the best—to appreciate humankind with its wonderful successes and hideous mistakes. We carry this appreciation and understanding of who we are and what we are capable of forward to yet another generation. Hopefully, among this group will be new historians to whom we can pass the torch and share this memory.

The careers outlined in this book and many, many others cry out for the human and farsighted, analytical perspective of the history major. The jobs have varying titles: archivist, interpreter, manager, dean of institutional research, curator, director of corporate planning, and a host of other titles. They all share the skills, the mental discipline, the orientation toward people and their behavior that help historians see events and decisions in perspective. Historians are critical and careful in their judgments and are able to talk and write about these events in ways that help others understand them and learn from them. Could we ask for anything more from a major?

History as Career Preparation

History is at the heart of the liberal arts, but unlike science or business, no standard curriculum exists, and a review of history curricula at colleges and universities across the country will display a dizzying variety of programs, including American History, Western Civilization, World History, Peace and War, and Diplomacy Studies.

But this major is more than just any one college's program of courses. I beyond the content of these selections. In fact, it cannot be mastered by ply mastering the courses within the curriculum. History is about making nections: across curriculums, nations, and racial, ethnic, and economic bc It is a way of looking at humankind, at events, at whatever task you ha front of you that requires analysis, perceptiveness, accuracy, curiosity, and

If you engage in your history degree fully, you will read volumin You'll learn to sift what you've read and think carefully and critically it. When you are ready with your own thinking about a topic, good p ration should have you ready to write authoritatively and accurately. This of clarity of thought is an excellent preparation for oral presentations. B all of this preparation will be solid grounding in research skills empha thoroughness, reliability, and ethics.

The relevance of history as an academic preparation for a career i dent in these skills, which are found enumerated in countless job pos some of which are threaded throughout this book and, in fact, throug all the volumes of the Great Jobs series. For history, more thoroughly any other of the liberal arts degrees, accomplishes two significant lea outcomes. First is technique: research, reading, analysis, writing, and s ing. Second is a greater appreciation of yourself and the human commu its wonderful diversity and expression.

The applicability and vitality of history as a career preparation are en if you take every advantage of your degree preparation. Most of the listed here require practice and sheer hard work. One can move pas through four years of a history degree, earn suitable grades, and acquire knowledge but learn very little. Or, you can test yourself continually in powers of research, reading, selectivity, and expression and engage you ulty in continual dialogue about the relevance and relationship of histo the present. This preferred second course is essential if you are to grad with any marketable skills, as a historian or in any other profession.

Knowledge of the past helps you to understand and engage in the ent, and you will draw upon your history course work again and again. Pe have a habit of repeating certain behaviors, and the repository of your n ory will awaken to similarities and connections between events in the and the present again and again.

History is not a set of mathematical formulae that are to be applie specific incidents for the correct results. History is humanity moving thr time and, depending on your vantage point, you see the lessons of hur ity from varying perspectives. Your age, race, time in life, country of or employment, and mood all have an effect on how you view and evaluat lessons history teaches you.

You learn about yourself in studying history. How you react to events, ple, and the choices they make is self-revealing. If you've been an assid- s history student, you may find the next chapter on self-assessment firming but not earth-shattering, as you have already faced many of these stions of interest, values, ethics, skills, and attributes in your studies. Your ing of history has been like a mirror held before you, reflecting back to nuch of who you truly are as you have grappled with the choices made 1ose you have studied.

elf-awareness also brings an appreciation for the diversity present in oth- 10t just those of our own cultural background, race, or milieu, but those 1tirely different surroundings, economics, and geography. History iden- and isolates those differences and makes them understandable while at 1me time giving a profound sense of the community of humankind. In sense, to truly study history is to inhabit the world of another and appre- and understand the superficial differences that separate us.

:ultural climates come to be understood, but the historian must also be :thing of a geographer to understand history and the impact of climate, in, and location. Certainly the self-imposed isolation of the Japanese re the arrival of Admiral Perry had political and geographic underpin- s. The isolation and the resultant dramatic opening of the country have left strong imprints on the homogeneity of Japanese culture.

1ace exploration, the atomic bomb, patent medicines, the automobile, irplane, penicillin, biological warfare, defoliants, and satellite commu- ions all have had historical significance and must be part of the history :nt's study. History's curriculum is loose because it shares all curriculums, depending upon the geography, people, events, or time you choose to /, you will need to become an art critic, sociologist, ethnomusicologist, met, weapons specialist, or cultural anthropologist. Often, with more ng effect than any war might have, the scientific and technological 1nces determine the course of history.

1ut for all the technological influences, history remains the province of 1n activity. The incredible response of the British citizenry during World II, an ethos that remains palpable in British society today among that ·ation, was fostered in large part by the role of the monarchy as arche- al family. King George VI and Queen Elizabeth (the mother of Queen beth II) kept their daughters in the country. Buckingham Palace took t bomb hits on the grounds and the King and Queen toured bombed in London, connecting directly with the populace. The Queen donated suites of household goods from royal estates to victims of the bombing. y of these gestures and more by the royal family were credited with keeping sh resolve and spunk high during the dark days of World War II.

The importance of history is not immediately apparent, even to those who are living some of its most memorable moments. History is a term we use in retrospect. Though the present is to become history immediately, we often need the wonderful filter and distance of time to appreciate and understand events, people, and their relationship. As you pursue your studies of history and consider some of the wonderful career possibilities it affords you, don't neglect other aspects of your education. If you can travel outside the country, do so. It will forever change your view of your own native land as you begin to see it as others do. Travel, read as much as you can, and don't limit your subject matter, because all human activity is grist for the mill of history.

Engage your teachers, classmates, and others in good discussions on current events, and test your awareness of the forces involved and your appreciation of how others view the same situation. Listen carefully and put yourself in someone else's shoes. Try on different opinions. Argue the other side and play the devil's advocate, and never forget that history is not fact, but considered opinion.

Peace is a desirable objective, but may not be realistic in historic terms. Look around at the other frontiers of history. Medicine moves along its curative path, only to be challenged by the mystery of AIDS and Alzheimer's disease. The situation of the homeless grows exponentially, not just in the United States, but around the world, and the gap between the haves and the have-nots widens perceptibly. The United States' reaction to the events of September 11, 2001, and the subsequent wars in Iraq and Afghanistan have led to new laws (and a continuing public debate) about the needs of national security versus the privacy rights of citizens, not to mention those who might be considered the nation's enemies.

Technology has brought opportunities and problems. Communications are more rapid than ever before, and yet we linger on automated voice mail, hoping to speak to a "real" person. Premature infants can be brought back from the brink of death to be sustained indefinitely on life support at phenomenal cost. Discretionary income allows for protected communities that resemble most closely medieval cities with the drawbridges drawn up against a hostile world.

As a student of history, this may sound pretty gloomy and make you wonder, "What can I do? How can I possibly help or make a difference?" The answers lie in the chapters that follow. Although many pundits do agree that we face serious domestic and global challenges, as individuals with an appreciation of the future as history, you can make a difference. Individual differences do count, because they are the beginnings of collective change.

Each of the career paths that this book suggests—archivists and curators; business, industry, and commerce workers and managers; teachers, both in and out of the formal school system; and information specialists—presents opportunities to affect our history. With your bachelor's degree and your appreciation of what makes history, you have the ability to hold up a stop sign at each important decision point in your career and say "consider the implications."

For the archivist and curator, there is the important opportunity of ensuring that the artifacts and records of the past are available and accessible to a public that needs to know the lessons of history. There will be ample opportunity, through exhibitions, catalogs, published articles, talks, and tours to make this information meaningful and real to the public. You'll want to consider the obstacles that have been placed between your collections and the public and the need for these obstacles. You will want to ensure the record you present is comprehensive and accurate. We are still working on historical rewriting of the role of women in history—always half the population but until recently not part of the story.

Those who choose to use their history degree in the world of commerce will have plenty of opportunities to humanize the history of their organization. Making facts and data relevant to the lives of the individuals involved, adding the human dimensions of business strategies and plans, and examining the impact on society for each business decision provide a succession of stop signs where one can consider the history and the consequences for the future.

Teachers in and out of the classroom have the gift of an audience and the techniques and tools to share history with people of all ages. In some cases, this might mean using costumes or oral performances to bring history to life. In others, it may involve accessing the Internet to illustrate a point being made in a classroom lecture.

Many of our decisions, plans, and ideas would have this consideration if we were able to retrieve and make use of existing records and documentation. Information specialists can be extraordinarily important in any organization if they position themselves not as technical librarians, whose only job is to store and produce information when requested, but as vital players in how an organization operates and plans for change. We are inundated with information, and the information specialist can be critical in sorting out the vital from the superfluous, directing pertinent data to the correct source, and anticipating data needs for good decision (and history) making.

So is this history? Absolutely. Remember Carl Becker's quote? History is the memory of things said and done. History is individual before it is collective, and history is the result of decisions made and not made. Knowing and believing that, what kind of history do you want to be remembered for in your career, and what will your contribution be to that history? Begin your exploration!

PART ONE

THE JOB SEARCH

1

The Self-Assessment

Self-assessment is the process by which you begin to acknowledge your own particular blend of education, experiences, values, needs, and goals. It provides the foundation for career planning and the entire job search process. Self-assessment involves looking inward and asking yourself what can sometimes prove to be difficult questions. This self-examination should lead to an intimate understanding of your personal traits and values, consumption patterns and economic needs, longer-term goals, skill base, preferred skills, and underdeveloped skills.

You come to the self-assessment process knowing yourself well in some of these areas, but you may still be uncertain about other aspects. You may be well aware of your consumption patterns, but have you spent much time specifically identifying your longer-term goals or your personal values as they relate to work? No matter what level of self-assessment you have undertaken to date, it is now time to clarify all of these issues and questions as they relate to the job search.

The knowledge you gain in the self-assessment process will guide the rest of your job search. In this book, you will learn about all of the following tasks:

- Writing résumés and cover letters
- Researching careers and networking
- Interviewing and job offer considerations

In each of these steps, you will rely on and often return to the understanding gained through your self-assessment. Any individual seeking employment must be able and willing to express these facets of his or her personality to recruiters and interviewers throughout the job search. This communication allows you to show the world who you are so that together with employers you can determine whether there will be a workable match with a given job or career path.

How to Conduct a Self-Assessment

The self-assessment process goes on naturally all the time. People ask you to clarify what you mean, you make a purchasing decision, or you begin a new relationship. You react to the world and the world reacts to you. How you understand these interactions and any changes you might make because of them are part of the natural process of self-discovery. There is, however, a more comprehensive and efficient way to approach self-assessment with regard to employment.

Because self-assessment can become a complex exercise, we have distilled it into a seven-step process that provides an effective basis for undertaking a job search. The seven steps include the following:

1. Understanding your personal traits
2. Identifying your personal values
3. Calculating your economic needs
4. Exploring your longer-term goals
5. Enumerating your skill base
6. Recognizing your preferred skills
7. Assessing skills needing further development

As you work through your self-assessment, you might want to create a worksheet similar to the one shown in Exhibit 1.1, starting on the following page. Or you might want to keep a journal of the thoughts you have as you undergo this process. There will be many opportunities to revise your self-assessment as you start down the path of seeking a career.

Step 1   Understand Your Personal Traits
Each person has a unique personality that he or she brings to the job search process. Gaining a better understanding of your personal traits can help you evaluate job and career choices. Identifying these traits and then finding employment that allows you to draw on at least some of them can create a rewarding and fulfilling work experience. If potential employment doesn't allow you to use these preferred traits, it is important to decide whether you

Exhibit 1.1
SELF-ASSESSMENT WORKSHEET

Step 1. Understand Your Personal Traits

The personal traits that describe me are
(Include all of the words that describe you.)
The ten personal traits that most accurately describe me are
(List these ten traits.)

Step 2. Identify Your Personal Values

Working conditions that are important to me include
*(List working conditions that would have to exist for you to accept a
position.)*
The values that go along with my working conditions are
(Write down the values that correspond to each working condition.)
Some additional values I've decided to include are
(List those values you identify as you conduct this job search.)

Step 3. Calculate Your Economic Needs

My estimated minimum annual salary requirement is
(Write the salary you have calculated based on your budget.)
Starting salaries for the positions I'm considering are
*(List the name of each job you are considering and the associated starting
salary.)*

Step 4. Explore Your Longer-Term Goals

My thoughts on longer-term goals right now are
(Jot down some of your longer-term goals as you know them right now.)

Step 5. Enumerate Your Skill Base

The general skills I possess are
(List the skills that underlie tasks you are able to complete.)
The specific skills I possess are
*(List more technical or specific skills that you possess, and indicate your level
of expertise.)*
General and specific skills that I want to promote to employers for the
jobs I'm considering are
(List general and specific skills for each type of job you are considering.)

continued

Step 6. Recognize Your Preferred Skills

Skills that I would like to use on the job include

(List skills that you hope to use on the job, and indicate how often you'd like to use them.)

Step 7. Assess Skills Needing Further Development

Some skills that I'll need to acquire for the jobs I'm considering include

(Write down skills listed in job advertisements or job descriptions that you don't currently possess.)

I believe I can build these skills by

(Describe how you plan to acquire these skills.)

---

can find other ways to express them or whether you would be better off not considering this type of job. Interests and hobbies pursued outside of work hours can be one way to use personal traits you don't have an opportunity to draw on in your work. For example, if you consider yourself an outgoing person and the kinds of jobs you are examining allow little contact with other people, you may be able to achieve the level of interaction that is comfortable for you outside of your work setting. If such a compromise seems impractical or otherwise unsatisfactory, you probably should explore only jobs that provide the interaction you want and need on the job.

Many young adults who are not very confident about their employability will downplay their need for income. They will say, "Money is not all that important if I love my work." But if you begin to document exactly what you need for housing, transportation, insurance, clothing, food, and utilities, you will begin to understand that some jobs cannot meet your financial needs and it doesn't matter how wonderful the job is. If you have to worry each payday about bills and other financial obligations, you won't be very effective on the job. Begin now to be honest with yourself about your needs.

Begin the self-assessment process by creating an inventory of your personal traits. Make a list of as many words as possible to describe yourself. Words like *accurate, creative, future-oriented, relaxed,* or *structured* are just a few examples. In addition, you might ask people who know you well how they might describe you.

Focus on Selected Personal Traits. Of all the traits you identified, select the ten you believe most accurately describe you. Keep track of these ten traits.

Consider Your Personal Traits in the Job Search Process. As you begin exploring jobs and careers, watch for matches between your personal traits and the job descriptions you read. Some jobs will require many personal traits you know you possess, and others will not seem to match those traits.

> A history writer's work, for example, requires an excellent grasp of the basics of written communication, including solid skills in grammar and usage as well as the ability to organize information so that it is clear and logical. Writers of historical materials must be able to summarize information, place it into proper context, and explain it so that it is understandable to readers. Their job requires an ability to take information from primary or secondary sources and adapt it to the type of material being written and the audience for whom it is intended, whether that is a high school or college textbook, a nonfiction book for younger readers, a brochure for a historical park, or explanatory displays in a museum. There may be a need to meet strict deadlines and to work cooperatively with editors or other writers.

Your ability to respond to changing conditions, your decision-making ability, productivity, creativity, and verbal skills all have a bearing on your success in and enjoyment of your work life. To better guarantee success, be sure to take the time needed to understand these traits in yourself.

Step 2   Identify Your Personal Values

Your personal values affect every aspect of your life, including employment, and they develop and change as you move through life. Values can be defined as principles that we hold in high regard, qualities that are important and desirable to us. Some values aren't ordinarily connected to work (love, beauty, color, light, relationships, family, or religion), and others are (autonomy, cooperation, effectiveness, achievement, knowledge, and security). Our values determine, in part, the level of satisfaction we feel in a particular job.

Define Acceptable Working Conditions. One facet of employment is the set of working conditions that must exist for someone to consider taking a job.

Each of us would probably create a unique list of acceptable working conditions, but items that might be included on many people's lists are the amount of money you would need to be paid, how far you are willing to drive or travel, the amount of freedom you want in determining your own schedule, whether you would be working with people or data or things, and the types of tasks you would be willing to do. Your conditions might include statements of working conditions you will *not* accept; for example, you might not be willing to work at night or on weekends or holidays.

If you were offered a job tomorrow, what conditions would have to exist for you to realistically consider accepting the position? Take some time and make a list of these conditions.

Realize Associated Values. Your list of working conditions can be used to create an inventory of your values relating to jobs and careers you are exploring. For example, if one of your conditions stated that you wanted to earn at least $30,000 per year, the associated value would be financial gain. If another condition was that you wanted to work with a friendly group of people, the value that went along with that might be belonging or interaction with people.

Relate Your Values to the World of Work. As you read the job descriptions you come across either in this book, in newspapers and magazines, or online, think about the values associated with each position.

For instance, the work of a museum director would include planning exhibits and developing schedules for changing them. Once exhibits are in place, the director must supervise efforts to maintain them and to promote them to the public.

At least some of the associated values in the field you're exploring should match those you extracted from your list of working conditions. Take a second look at any values that don't match up. How important are they to you? What will happen if they are not satisfied on the job? Can you incorporate those personal values elsewhere? Your answers need to be brutally honest. As you continue your exploration, be sure to add to your list any additional values that occur to you.

Step 3   Calculate Your Economic Needs

Each of us grew up in an environment that provided for certain basic needs, such as food and shelter, and, to varying degrees, other needs that we now consider basic, such as cable television, e-mail, or an automobile. Needs such as privacy, space, and quiet, which at first glance may not appear to be monetary needs, may add to housing expenses and so should be considered as you examine your economic needs. For example, if you place a high value on a large, open living space for yourself, it would be difficult to satisfy that need without an associated high housing cost, especially in a densely populated city environment.

As you prepare to move into the world of work and become responsible for meeting your own basic needs, it is important to consider the salary you will need to be able to afford a satisfying standard of living. The three-step process outlined here will help you plan a budget, which in turn will allow you to evaluate the various career choices and geographic locations you are considering. The steps include (1) develop a realistic budget, (2) examine starting salaries, and (3) use a cost-of-living index.

Develop a Realistic Budget. Each of us has certain expectations for the kind of lifestyle we want to maintain. To begin the process of defining your economic needs, it will be helpful to determine what you expect to spend on routine monthly expenses. These expenses include housing, food, transportation, entertainment, utilities, loan repayments, and revolving charge accounts. You may not currently spend anything for certain items, but you probably will have to once you begin supporting yourself. As you develop this budget, be generous in your estimates, but keep in mind any items that could be reduced or eliminated. If you are not sure about the cost of a certain item, talk with family or friends who would be able to give you a realistic estimate.

If this is new or difficult for you, start to keep a log of expenses right now. You may be surprised at how much you actually spend each month for food or stamps or magazines. Household expenses and personal grooming items can often loom very large in a budget, as can auto repairs or home maintenance.

Income taxes must also be taken into consideration when examining salary requirements. State and local taxes vary, so it is difficult to calculate exactly the effect of taxes on the amount of income you need to generate. To roughly estimate the gross income necessary to generate your minimum annual salary requirement, multiply the minimum salary you have calculated by a factor of 1.35. The resulting figure will be an approximation of what your gross income would need to be, given your estimated expenses.

Examine Starting Salaries. Starting salaries for each of the career tracks are provided throughout this book. These salary figures can be used in conjunction with the cost-of-living index (discussed in the next section) to determine whether you would be able to meet your basic economic needs in a given geographic location.

Use a Cost-of-Living Index. If you are thinking about trying to get a job in a geographic region other than the one where you now live, understanding differences in the cost of living will help you come to a more informed decision about making a move. By using a cost-of-living index, you can compare salaries offered and the cost of living in different locations with what you know about the salaries offered and the cost of living in your present location.

Many variables are used to calculate the cost-of-living index. Often included are housing, groceries, utilities, transportation, health care, clothing, and entertainment expenses. Right now you do not need to worry about the details associated with calculating a given index. The main purpose of this exercise is to help you understand that pay ranges for entry-level positions may not vary greatly, but the cost of living in different locations *can* vary tremendously.

If you lived in Bloomington, Indiana, for example, and you were interested in working as an associate editor at a consumer history magazine, you might find that you would earn $35,000 annually. But let's say you're also thinking about moving to Los Angeles, Miami, or Charlotte, North Carolina. You know you can live on $35,000 in Bloomington, but you want to be able to equal that salary in the other locations you're considering. How much will you have to earn in those locations to do this? Determining the cost of living for each city will show you. Many websites, such as DataMasters (datamasters.com) can assist you as you undertake this research. Or use any search engine and enter the keywords "cost of living index." Several choices will appear. Choose one site and look for options such as cost-of-living analysis or cost-of-living comparator. Some sites will ask you to register and/or pay for the information, but most sites are free. Follow the instructions provided and you will be able to create a table of information like the one shown here. At the time this com-

Job: Assistant Editor

City	Base Amount	Equivalent Salary
Bloomington, IN	$35,000	
Los Angeles, CA		$58,207
Miami, FL		$50,217
Charlotte, NC		$33,478

parison was done, you would have needed to earn $58,207 in Los Angeles, $50,217 in Miami or just $33,478 in Charlotte to match the buying power of $35,000 in Bloomington.

If you moved to Charlotte and secured employment as an associate editor with the same salary earned in Bloomington, you would be able to maintain a lifestyle similar to the one you led in Indiana. In fact, you would be able to enhance your lifestyle very modestly given the slight increase in buying power. On the other hand, moving to Miami from Bloomington would significantly decrease your buying power unless your new salary was at least $50,000. And without a large increase (to at least $58,000), moving to Los Angeles would mean a more drastic change in your buying power. Remember, these figures change all the time, so be sure to undertake your own calculations. If you would like to see how the figures were calculated, visit the DataMasters website or check out other sites that provide cost of living comparisons.

You can work through a similar exercise for any type of job you are considering and for many locations when current salary information is available. It will be worth your time to undertake this analysis if you are seriously considering a relocation. By doing so you will be able to make an informed choice.

Step 4   Explore Your Longer-Term Goals

There is no question that when we first begin working, our goals are to use our skills and education in a job that will reward us with employment, income, and status relative to the preparation we brought with us to this position. If we are not being paid as much as we feel we should for our level of education or if job demands don't provide the intellectual stimulation we had hoped for, we experience unhappiness and as a result often seek other employment.

Most jobs we consider "good" are those that fulfill our basic "lower-level" needs of security, food, clothing, shelter, income, and productive work. But even when our basic needs are met and our jobs are secure and productive, we as individuals are constantly changing. As we change, the demands and expectations we place on our jobs may change. Fortunately, some jobs grow and change with us, and this explains why some people are happy throughout many years in a job.

But more often people are bigger than the jobs they fill. We have more goals and needs than any job could satisfy. These are "higher-level" needs of self-esteem, companionship, affection, and an increasing desire to feel we are employing ourselves in the most effective way possible. Not all of these higher-level needs can be met through employment, but for as long as we are employed, we increasingly demand that our jobs play their part in moving us along the path to fulfillment.

Another obvious but important fact is that we change as we mature. Although our jobs also have the potential for change, they may not change as frequently or as markedly as we do. There are increasingly fewer one-job, one-employer careers; we must think about a work future that may involve voluntary or forced moves from employer to employer. Because of that very real possibility, we need to take advantage of the opportunities in each position we hold. Acquiring the skills and competencies associated with each position will keep us viable and attractive as employees. This is particularly true in a job market that not only is technology/computer dependent, but also is populated with more and more small, self-transforming organizations rather than the large, seemingly stable organizations of the past.

If you are considering the possibility of a position teaching high school history, for example, you would gain a better perspective of your potential future if you could talk to a first-year or second-year instructor, a more experienced teacher, and finally a principal or other administrator with significant experience in hiring and supervising history teachers. Each person will have a different experience and outlook and may provide invaluable advice.

Step 5 Enumerate Your Skill Base

In terms of the job search, skills can be thought of as capabilities that can be developed in school, at work, or by volunteering and then used in specific job settings. Many studies have documented the kinds of skills that employers seek in entry-level applicants. For example, some of the most desired skills for individuals interested in the teaching profession are the ability to interact effectively with students one-on-one, to manage a classroom, to adapt to varying situations as necessary, and to get involved in school activities. Business employers have also identified important qualities, including enthusiasm for the employer's product or service, a businesslike mind, the ability to follow written or oral instructions, the ability to demonstrate self-control, the confidence to suggest new ideas, the ability to communicate with all members of a group, an awareness of cultural differences, and loyalty, to name just a few. You will find that many of these skills are also in the repertoire of qualities demanded in your college major.

To be successful in obtaining any given job, you must be able to demonstrate that you possess a certain mix of skills that will allow you to carry out the duties required by that job. This skill mix will vary a great deal from job to job; to determine the skills necessary for the jobs you are seeking, you can read job advertisements or more generic job descriptions, such as those found later in this book. If you want to be effective in the job search, you must directly show employers that you possess the skills needed to be successful in filling the position. These skills will initially be described on your résumé and then discussed again during the interview process.

Skills are either general or specific. To develop a list of skills relevant to employers, you must first identify the general skills you possess, then list specific skills you have to offer, and, finally, examine which of these skills employers are seeking.

Identify Your General Skills. Because you possess or will possess a college degree, employers will assume that you can read and write, perform certain basic computations, think critically, and communicate effectively. Employers will want to see that you have acquired these skills, and they will want to know which additional general skills you possess.

One way to begin identifying skills is to write an experiential diary. An experiential diary lists all the tasks you were responsible for completing for each job you've held and then outlines the skills required to do those tasks. You may list several skills for any given task. This diary allows you to distinguish between the tasks you performed and the underlying skills required to complete those tasks. Here's an example:

Tasks	Skills
Answering telephone	Effective use of language, clear diction, ability to direct inquiries, ability to solve problems
Waiting on tables	Poise under conditions of time and pressure, speed, accuracy, good memory, simultaneous completion of tasks, sales skills

For each job or experience you have participated in, develop a worksheet based on the example shown here. On a résumé, you may want to describe these skills rather than simply listing tasks. Skills are easier for the employer to appreciate, especially when your experience is very different from the employment you are seeking. In addition to helping you identify general skills, this experiential diary will prepare you to speak more effectively in an interview about the qualifications you possess.

Identify Your Specific Skills. It may be easier to identify your specific skills because you can definitely say whether you can speak other languages, program a computer, draft a map or diagram, or edit a document using appropriate symbols and terminology.

Using your experiential diary, identify the points in your history where you learned how to do something very specific, and decide whether you have a beginning, intermediate, or advanced knowledge of how to use that particular skill. Right now, be sure to list *every* specific skill you have, and don't consider whether you like using the skill. Write down a list of specific skills you have acquired and the level of competence you possess—beginning, intermediate, or advanced.

Relate Your Skills to Employers. You probably have thought about a couple of different jobs you might be interested in obtaining, and one way to begin relating the general and specific skills you possess to a potential employer's needs is to read actual advertisements for these types of positions (see Part Two for resources listing actual job openings).

For example, you might be interested in beginning your career as an educational program specialist, focusing on developing history education programs for the general public. A job listing might read, "Initiate/design/produce history-related educational programs. Requires degree in history or substantial course work in the field, excellent writing skills, communication/presentation skills, word-processing capabilities." If you then used any one of a number of general sources of information that describe the job of educational program specialist, you would find additional information. Specialists in this area might develop course outlines, write scripts, prepare informational materials, and search sources.

Begin building a comprehensive list of required skills with the first job description you read. Exploring advertisements for and descriptions of several types of related positions will reveal an important core of skills that are necessary for obtaining the type of work you're interested in. In building this list, include both general and specific skills.

The following is a sample list of skills needed to be successful as an educational program specialist. These items were extracted from both general resources and actual job listings.

Job: Educational Program Specialist

General Skills	**Specific Skills**
Review historical documents	Summarize historical information
Perform interviews	Analyze historical trends
Draft course materials	Travel domestically
Draft correspondence	Develop course outlines
Prepare course outlines	Write scripts
Conduct studies	Develop course supplements
Search sources	Communicate effectively
Use computer	Develop exhibits
Present information orally	Use phone extensively
Answer inquiries	Keep written records
	Work under pressure
	Track down sources
	Conduct oral interviews

On separate sheets of paper, try to generate a comprehensive list of required skills for at least one job you are considering.

The list of general skills that you develop for a given career path will be valuable for any number of jobs you might apply for. Many of the specific skills would also be transferable to other types of positions. For example, writing informational materials is a required skill for many positions.

Step 6   Recognize Your Preferred Skills

In the previous section you developed a comprehensive list of skills that relate to particular career paths that are of interest to you. You can now relate these to skills that you prefer to use. We all use a wide range of skills (some researchers say individuals have a repertoire of about five hundred skills), but we may not particularly be interested in using all of them in our work. There may be some skills that come to us more naturally or that we use successfully time and time again and that we want to continue to use; these are best described as our preferred skills. For this exercise use the list of skills that you created for the previous section, and decide which of them you are *most interested in using* in future work and how often you would like to use them. You might be interested in using some skills only occasionally, while others you would like to use more regularly. You probably also have skills that you hope you can use constantly.

As you examine job announcements, look for matches between this list of preferred skills and the qualifications described in the advertisements. These skills should be highlighted on your résumé and discussed in job interviews.

Step 7   Assess Skills Needing Further Development

Previously you compiled a list of general and specific skills required for given positions. You already possess some of these skills; those that remain to be developed are your underdeveloped skills.

If you are just beginning the job search, there may be gaps between the qualifications required for some of the jobs you're considering and the skills you possess. The thought of having to admit to and talk about these underdeveloped skills, especially in a job interview, is a frightening one. One way to put a healthy perspective on this subject is to target and relate your exploration of underdeveloped skills to the types of positions you are seeking. Recognizing these shortcomings and planning to overcome them with either on-the-job training or additional formal education can be a positive way to address the concept of underdeveloped skills.

On your worksheet or in your journal, make a list of up to five general or specific skills required for the positions you're interested in that you *don't currently possess*. For each item list an idea you have for specific action you could take to acquire that skill. Do some brainstorming to come up with possible actions. If you have a hard time generating ideas, talk to people currently working in this type of position, professionals in your college career services office, trusted friends, family members, or members of related professional associations.

In the chapter on interviewing, we will discuss in detail how to effectively address questions about underdeveloped skills. Generally speaking, though, employers want genuine answers to these types of questions. They want you to reveal "the real you," and they also want to see how you answer difficult questions. In taking the positive, targeted approach discussed previously, you show the employer that you are willing to continue to learn and that you have a plan for strengthening your job qualifications.

Use Your Self-Assessment

Exploring entry-level career options can be an exciting experience if you have good resources available and will take the time to use them. Can you effectively complete the following tasks?

1. Understand your personality traits and relate them to career choices
2. Define your personal values
3. Determine your economic needs
4. Explore longer-term goals
5. Understand your skill base
6. Recognize your preferred skills
7. Express a willingness to improve on your underdeveloped skills

If so, then you can more meaningfully participate in the job search process by writing a more effective résumé, finding job titles that represent work you are interested in doing, locating job sites that will provide the opportunity for you to use your strengths and skills, networking in an informed way, participating in focused interviews, getting the most out of follow-up contacts, and evaluating job offers to find those that create a good match between you and the employer. The remaining chapters in Part One guide you through these next steps in the job search process. For many job seekers, this process can take anywhere from three months to a year to implement. The time you will need to put into your job search will depend on the type of job you want and the geographic location where you'd like to work. Think of your effort as a job in itself, requiring you to set aside time each week to complete the needed work. Carefully undertaken efforts may reduce the time you need for your job search.

2

The Résumé and Cover Letter

The task of writing a résumé may seem overwhelming if you are unfamiliar with this type of document, but there are some easily understood techniques that can and should be used. This section was written to help you understand the purpose of the résumé, the different types of formats available, and how to write the sections that contain information traditionally found on a résumé. We will present examples and explanations that address questions frequently posed by people writing their first résumé or updating an old one.

Even within the formats and suggestions given, however, there are infinite variations. True, most follow one of the outlines suggested, but you should feel free to adjust the résumé to suit your needs and make it expressive of your life and experience.

Why Write a Résumé?

The purpose of a résumé is to convince an employer that you should be interviewed. Whether you're mailing, faxing, or e-mailing this document, you'll want to present enough information to show that you can make an immediate and valuable contribution to an organization. A résumé is not an in-depth historical or legal document; later in the job search process you may be asked to document your entire work history on an application form and attest to its validity. The résumé should, instead, highlight relevant information pertaining directly to the organization that will receive the document or to the type of position you are seeking.

We will discuss the chronological and digital résumés in detail here. Functional and targeted résumés, which are used much less often, are briefly discussed. The reasons for using one type of résumé over another and the typical format for each are addressed in the following sections.

The Chronological Résumé

The chronological résumé is the most common of the various résumé formats and therefore the format that employers are most used to receiving. This type of résumé is easy to read and understand because it details the chronological progression of jobs you have held. (See Exhibit 2.1.) It begins with your most recent employment and works back in time. If you have a solid work history or have experience that provided growth and development in your duties and responsibilities, a chronological résumé will highlight these achievements. The typical elements of a chronological résumé include the heading, a career objective, educational background, employment experience, activities, and references.

The Heading
The heading consists of your name, address, telephone number, and other means of contact. This may include a fax number, e-mail address, and your home-page address. If you are using a shared e-mail account or a parent's business fax, be sure to let others who use these systems know that you may receive important professional correspondence via these systems. You wouldn't want to miss a vital e-mail or fax! Likewise, if your résumé directs readers to a personal home page on the Web, be certain it's a professional personal home page designed to be viewed and appreciated by a prospective employer. This may mean making substantial changes in the home page you currently mount on the Web.

The Objective
Without a doubt the objective statement is the most challenging part of the résumé for most writers. Even for individuals who have decided on a career path, it can be difficult to encapsulate all they want to say in one or two brief sentences. For job seekers who are unfocused or unclear about their intentions, trying to write this section can inhibit the entire résumé writing process.

Keep the objective as short as possible and no longer than two short sentences.

Exhibit 2.1
CHRONOLOGICAL RÉSUMÉ

LESLIE FAIRCHILD

218 Wade Hall
George Washington University
Washington, DC 20037
(202) 555-6666
ajones@xxx.com
(until May 2008)

127 Island Street
Dublin, VA 24084
(540) 555-4377

OBJECTIVE
History Museum Education Coordinator

EDUCATION
Bachelor of Arts in History
George Washington University
Concentration: Colonial American History
Minor: Mass Communications

HONORS/AWARDS
Dean's List, 2006, 2007
Distinguished Student Orientation Guide Award, 2006
Phi Delta Kappa Honor Society

RELATED COURSES
Interactive Technology Systems   Speech
American Art Traditions   Archaeology

EXPERIENCE
Orientation Leader, George Washington. 2006–2007.
Selected to be part of a special unit of students charged with orienting new
    students to the history, geography, and structure of the university. Large
    group sessions and smaller interactive program responsibilities. Trained new
    orientation leaders.

Interpreter/Guide, Jamestown Settlement, Williamsburg, VA.
Summers 2005, 2006, 2007.
Progressively greater responsibilities in a number of different settings as a
    costumed historic interpreter for this popular year-round historic site.
    Specific training in early-American gardens, import china, and furnishings.

continued

Student Assistant, History Department, George Washington University. Part-time, 2006–2007.
A recurring work study position assisting history faculty in test preparation, special event planning, history film series organization, and student library cataloguing and maintenance. Answered inquiries from history students and other staff.

ACTIVITIES
American History Club, active member, 2006–present.
Colonial Forum participant, 2004–present.
Virginia Constitution Conference student team assistant, 2006.

REFERENCES
Available upon request.

Choose one of the following types of objective statement:

1. General Objective Statement

- An entry-level educational programming coordinator position

2. Position-Focused Objective

- To obtain the position of conference coordinator at State College

3. Industry-Focused Objective

- To begin a career as a sales representative in the cruise line industry

4. Summary of Qualifications Statement

My three years of experience in preservation of historic buildings and my part-time employment in retail management have prepared me to take on the added responsibilities of a supervisory role in historic preservation.

Support Your Objective. A résumé that contains any one of these types of objective statements should then go on to demonstrate why you are qualified to get the position. Listing academic degrees can be one way to indicate qualifications. Another demonstration would be in the way previous experiences, both volunteer and paid, are described. Without this kind of documentation in the body of the résumé, the objective looks unsupported. Think of the résumé as telling a connected story about you. All the elements should work together to form a coherent picture that ideally should relate to your statement of objective.

Education

This section of your résumé should indicate the exact name of the degree you will receive or have received, spelled out completely with no abbreviations. The degree is generally listed after the objective, followed by the institution name and location, and then the month and year of graduation. This section could also include your academic minor, grade point average (GPA), and appearance on the Dean's List or President's List.

If you have enough space, you might want to include a section listing courses related to the field in which you are seeking work. The best use of a "related courses" section would be to list some course work that is not traditionally associated with the major. Perhaps you took several computer courses outside your degree that will be helpful and related to the job prospects you are entertaining. Several education section examples are shown here:

- BA in history with a minor in political science; University of Tennessee, Knoxville, TN; May 2008
- Bachelor of arts degree in history; Bluefield State College, Bluefield, WV; May 2007; Concentration: Asian history and culture

An example of a format for a related courses section follows:

RELATED COURSES

Public Relations	Web Design
Business Writing	Desktop Publishing
Public Speaking	Expository Writing
Research Methods	

Experience

The experience section of your résumé should be the most substantial part and should take up most of the space on the page. Employers want to see what kind of work history you have. They will look at your range of experiences, longevity in jobs, and specific tasks you are able to complete. This section may also be called "work experience," "related experience," "employment history," or "employment." No matter what you call this section, some important points to remember are the following:

1. **Describe your duties** as they relate to the position you are seeking.
2. **Emphasize major responsibilities** and indicate increases in responsibility. Include all relevant employment experiences: summer, part-time, internships, cooperative education, or self-employment.
3. **Emphasize skills**, especially those that transfer from one situation to another. The fact that you coordinated a student organization, chaired meetings, supervised others, and managed a budget leads one to suspect that you could coordinate other things as well.
4. **Use descriptive job titles** that provide information about what you did. A "Student Intern" should be more specifically stated as, for example, "Magazine Operations Intern." "Volunteer" is also too general; a title such as "Peer Writing Tutor" would be more appropriate.
5. **Create word pictures** by using active verbs to start sentences. Describe *results* you have produced in the work you have done.

A limp description would say something such as the following: "My duties included helping with production, proofreading, and editing. I used a design and page layout program." An action statement would be stated as follows: "Coordinated and assisted in the creative marketing of brochures and seminar promotions, becoming proficient in Quark."

Remember, an accomplishment is simply a result, a final measurable product that people can relate to. A duty is not a result; it is an obligation— every job holder has duties. For an effective résumé, list as many results as you can. To make the most of the limited space you have and to give your description impact, carefully select appropriate and accurate descriptors.

Here are some traits that employers tell us they like to see:

- Teamwork
- Energy and motivation

- Learning and using new skills
- Versatility
- Critical thinking
- Understanding how profits are created
- Organizational acumen
- Communicating directly and clearly, in both writing and speaking
- Risk taking
- Willingness to admit mistakes
- High personal standards

Solutions to Frequently Encountered Problems

Repetitive Employment with the Same Employer
EMPLOYMENT: The Foot Locker, Portland, Oregon. Summer 2001, 2002, 2003. Initially employed in high school as salesclerk. Because of successful performance, asked to return next two summers at higher pay with added responsibility. Ranked as the #2 salesperson the first summer and #1 the next two summers. Assisted in arranging eye-catching retail displays; served as manager of other summer workers during owner's absence.

A Large Number of Jobs
EMPLOYMENT: Recent Hospitality Industry Experience: Affiliated with four upscale hotel/restaurant complexes (September 2001–February 2004), where I worked part- and full-time as a waiter, bartender, disc jockey, and bookkeeper to produce income for college.

Several Positions with the Same Employer
EMPLOYMENT: Coca-Cola Bottling Co., Burlington, Vermont, 2001–2004. In four years, I received three promotions, each with increased pay and responsibility.

Summer Sales Coordinator: Promoted to hire, train, and direct efforts of add-on staff of fifteen college-age route salespeople hired to meet summer peak demand for product.

Sales Administrator: Promoted to run home office sales desk, managing accounts and associated delivery schedules for professional sales force of ten people. Intensive phone work, daily interaction with all personnel, and strong knowledge of product line required.

Route Salesperson: Summer employment to travel and tourism industry sites that use Coke products. Met specific schedule demands, used good communication skills with wide variety of customers, and demonstrated strong selling skills. Named salesperson of the month for July and August of that year.

Questions Résumé Writers Often Ask

How Far Back Should I Go in Terms of Listing Past Jobs?
Usually, listing three or four jobs should suffice. If you did something back in high school that has a bearing on your future aspirations for employment, by all means list the job. As you progress through your college career, high school jobs will be replaced on the résumé by college employment.

Should I Differentiate Between Paid and Nonpaid Employment?
Most employers are not initially concerned about how much you were paid. They are eager to know how much responsibility you held in your past employment. There is no need to specify that your work was as a volunteer if you had significant responsibilities.

How Should I Represent My Accomplishments or Work-Related Responsibilities?
Succinctly, but fully. In other words, give the employer enough information to arouse curiosity but not so much detail that you leave nothing to the imagination. Besides, some jobs merit more lengthy explanations than others. Be sure to convey any information that can give an employer a better understanding of the depth of your involvement at work. Did you supervise others? How many? Did your efforts result in a more efficient operation? How much did you increase efficiency? Did you handle a budget? How much? Were you promoted in a short time? Did you work two jobs at once or fifteen hours per week after high school? Where appropriate, quantify.

Should the Work Section Always Follow the Education Section on the Résumé?
Always lead with your strengths. If your education closely relates to the employment you now seek, put this section after the objective. If your

education does not closely relate but you have a surplus of good work experiences, consider reversing the order of your sections to lead with employment, followed by education.

How Should I Present My Activities, Honors, Awards, Professional Societies, and Affiliations?

This section of the résumé can add valuable information for an employer to consider if used correctly. The rule of thumb for information in this section is to include only those activities that are in some way relevant to the objective stated on your résumé. If you can draw a valid connection between your activities and your objective, include them; if not, leave them out.

Professional affiliations and honors should all be listed; especially important are those related to your job objective. Social clubs and activities need not be a part of your résumé unless you hold a significant office or you are looking for a position related to your membership. Be aware that most prospective employers' principal concerns are related to your employability, not your social life. If you have any, publications can be included as an addendum to your résumé.

How Should I Handle References?

The use of references is considered a part of the interview process, and they should never be listed on a résumé. You would always provide references to a potential employer if requested to, so it is not even necessary to include this section on the résumé if space does not permit. If space is available, it is acceptable to include the following statement:

- References furnished upon request.

The Functional Résumé

A functional résumé departs from a chronological résumé in that it organizes information by specific accomplishments in various settings: previous jobs, volunteer work, associations, and so forth. This type of résumé permits you to stress the substance of your experiences rather than the position titles you have held. You should consider using a functional résumé if you have held a series of similar jobs that relied on the same skills or abilities. There are many good books in which you can find examples of functional résumés, including *How to Write a Winning Resume* or *Resumes Made Easy*.

The Targeted Résumé

The targeted résumé focuses on specific work-related capabilities you can bring to a given position within an organization. Past achievements are listed to highlight your capabilities and the work history section is abbreviated.

Digital Résumés

Today's employers have to manage an enormous number of résumés. One of the most frequent complaints the writers of this series hear from students is the failure of employers to even acknowledge the receipt of a résumé and cover letter. Frequently, the reason for this poor response or nonresponse is the volume of applications received for every job. In an attempt to better manage the considerable labor investment involved in processing large numbers of résumés, many employers are requiring digital submission of résumés. There are two types of digital résumés: those that can be e-mailed or posted to a website, called *electronic résumés*, and those that can be "read" by a computer, commonly called *scannable résumés*. Though the format may be a bit different from the traditional "paper" résumé, the goal of both types of digital résumés is the same—to get you an interview! These résumés must be designed to be "technologically friendly." What that basically means to you is that they should be free of graphics and fancy formatting. (See Exhibit 2.2.)

Electronic Résumés

Sometimes referred to as plain-text résumés, electronic résumés are designed to be e-mailed to an employer or posted to one of many commercial Internet databases such as Careerbuilder.com, America's Job Bank (ajb.dni.us), or Monster.com.

Some technical considerations:

- Electronic résumés must be written in American Standard Code for Information Interchange (ASCII), which is simply a plain-text format. These characters are universally recognized so that every computer can accurately read and understand them. To create an ASCII file of your current résumé, open your document, then save it as a text or ASCII file. This will eliminate all formatting. Edit as needed using your computer's text editor application.
- Use a standard-width typeface. Courier is a good choice because it is the font associated with ASCII in most systems.

Exhibit 2.2
DIGITAL RÉSUMÉ

ROBIN E. PEREZ
443 Rio Silado Drive
Austin, TX 78767
(512) 555-7745
robinp@xxx.net

Put your name at the top on its own line.

Put your phone number on its own line.

KEYWORD SUMMARY
Certified State of Texas, secondary education
Passed PRAXIS exam
Fluent in English, Spanish
Political campaign experience
Writing/editing experience

Keywords make your résumé easier to find in a database.

EDUCATION
Bachelor of Arts, History, 2007
University of Texas
Minor: Political Science
G.P.A.: 3.8/4.0

Use a standard-width typeface.

RELATED COURSES
American Diplomacy, Modern Political Thought
History of the Americas, Colonial History
Computer Applications in the Social Sciences

No line should exceed 65 characters.

EXPERIENCE
Intern, Texas Department of Culture, Summer 2005
Organized displays, wrote and designed newsletters, maintained files

Capitalize letters to emphasize heading.

Customer Service Representative, Keystone
Incorporated, Austin, Texas, Summer 2006 and 2007
Made courtesy calls to customers, responded to
requests for assistance, resolved customer complaints

End each line by hitting the ENTER (or RETURN) key.

continued

Volunteer campaign worker
Office of Senator Joshua Robertson, 6th Senatorial District
Assisted in developing campaign literature, manned
telephone banks, assisted in developing newsletters and flyers

REFERENCES
Available on request.
++Willing to relocate++

- Use a font size of 11 to 14 points. A 12-point font is considered standard.
- Your margin should be left-justified.
- Do not exceed sixty-five characters per line because the word-wrap function doesn't operate in ASCII.
- Do not use boldface, italics, underlining, bullets, or various font sizes. Instead, use asterisks, plus signs, or all capital letters when you want to emphasize something.
- Avoid graphics and shading.
- Use as many "keywords" as you possibly can. These are words or phrases usually relating to skills or experience that either are specifically used in the job announcement or are popular buzzwords in the industry.
- Minimize abbreviations.
- Your name should be the first line of text.
- Conduct a "test run" by e-mailing your résumé to yourself and a friend before you send it to the employer. See how it transmits, and make any changes you need to. Continue to test it until it's exactly how you want it to look.
- Unless an employer specifically requests that you send the résumé in the form of an attachment, don't. Employers can encounter problems opening a document as an attachment, and there are always viruses to consider.
- Don't forget your cover letter. Send it along with your résumé as a single message.

Scannable Résumés

Some companies are relying on technology to narrow the candidate pool for available job openings. Electronic Applicant Tracking uses imaging to scan, sort, and store résumé elements in a database. Then, through OCR (Optical Character Recognition) software, the computer scans the résumés for keywords and phrases. To have the best chance at getting an interview, you want to increase the number of "hits"—matches of your skills, abilities, experience, and education to those the computer is scanning for—your résumé will get. You can see how critical using the right keywords is for this type of résumé.

Technical considerations include:

- Again, do not use boldface (newer systems may be able to read this, but many older ones won't), italics, underlining, bullets, shading, graphics, or multiple font sizes. Instead, for emphasis, use asterisks, plus signs, or all capital letters. Minimize abbreviations.
- Use a popular typeface such as Courier, Helvetica, Arial, or Palatino. Avoid decorative fonts.
- Font size should be between 11 and 14 points.
- Do not compress the spacing between letters.
- Use horizontal and vertical lines sparingly; the computer may misread them as the letters *L* or *I*.
- Left-justify the text.
- Do not use parentheses or brackets around telephone numbers, and be sure your phone number is on its own line of text.
- Your name should be the first line of text and on its own line. If your résumé is longer than one page, be sure to put your name on the top of all pages.
- Use a traditional résumé structure. The chronological format may work best.
- Use nouns that are skill-focused, such as *management, writer,* and *programming.* This is different from traditional paper résumés, which use action-oriented verbs.
- Laser printers produce the finest copies. Avoid dot-matrix printers.
- Use standard, light-colored paper with text on one side only. Since the higher the contrast, the better, your best choice is black ink on white paper.
- Always send original copies. If you must fax, set the fax on fine mode, not standard.
- Do not staple or fold your résumé. This can confuse the computer.
- Before you send your scannable résumé, be certain the employer uses this technology. If you can't determine this, you may want to send two versions (scannable and traditional) to be sure your résumé gets considered.

Résumé Production and Other Tips

An ink-jet printer is the preferred option for printing your résumé. Begin by printing just a few copies. You may find a small error or you may simply want to make some changes, and it is less frustrating and less expensive if you print in small batches.

Résumé paper color should be carefully chosen. You should consider the types of employers who will receive your résumé and the types of positions for which you are applying. Use white or ivory paper for traditional or conservative employers or for higher-level positions.

Black ink on sharp, white paper can be harsh on the reader's eyes. Think about an ivory or cream paper that will provide less contrast and be easier to read. Pink, green, and blue tints should generally be avoided.

Many résumé writers buy packages of matching envelopes and cover sheet stationery that, although not absolutely necessary, help convey a professional impression.

If you'll be producing many cover letters at home, be sure you have high-quality printing equipment. Learn standard envelope formats for business, and retain a copy of every cover letter you send out. You can use the copies to take notes of any telephone conversations that may occur.

If attending a job fair, either carry a briefcase or place your résumé in a nicely covered legal-size pad holder.

The Cover Letter

The cover letter provides you with the opportunity to tailor your résumé by telling the prospective employer how you can be a benefit to the organization. It allows you to highlight aspects of your background that are not already discussed in your résumé and that might be especially relevant to the organization you are contacting or to the position you are seeking. Every résumé should have a cover letter enclosed when you send it out. Unlike the résumé, which may be mass-produced, a cover letter is most effective when it is individually prepared and focused on the particular requirements of the organization in question.

A good cover letter should supplement the résumé and motivate the reader to review the résumé. The format shown in Exhibit 2.3 (see page 34) is only a suggestion to help you decide what information to include in a cover letter.

Begin the cover letter with your street address six lines down from the top. Leave three to five lines between the date and the name of the person to whom you are addressing the cover letter. Make sure you leave one blank line between the salutation and the body of the letter and between paragraphs. After typing "Sincerely," leave four blank lines and type your name. This should leave plenty of room for your signature. A sample cover letter is shown in Exhibit 2.4 on page 35.

The following guidelines will help you write good cover letters:

1. Be sure to type your letter neatly; ensure there are no misspellings.
2. Avoid unusual typefaces, such as script.
3. Address the letter to an individual, using the person's name and title. To obtain this information, call the company. If answering a blind newspaper advertisement, address the letter "To Whom It May Concern" or omit the salutation.
4. Be sure your cover letter directly indicates the position you are applying for and tells why you are qualified to fill it.
5. Send the original letter, not a photocopy, with your résumé. Keep a copy for your records.
6. Make your cover letter no more than one page.
7. Include a phone number where you can be reached.
8. Avoid trite language and have someone read the letter over to react to its tone, content, and mechanics.
9. For your own information, record the date you send out each letter and résumé.

Exhibit 2.3
COVER LETTER FORMAT

Your Street Address
Your Town, State, Zip
Phone Number
Fax Number
E-mail

Date

Name
Title
Organization
Address

Dear _____:

First Paragraph. In this paragraph state the reason for the letter, name the specific position or type of work you are applying for, and indicate from which resource (career services office, website, newspaper, contact, employment service) you learned of this opening. The first paragraph can also be used to inquire about future openings.

Second Paragraph. Indicate why you are interested in this position, the company, or its products or services and what you can do for the employer. If you are a recent graduate, explain how your academic background makes you a qualified candidate. Try not to repeat the same information found in the résumé.

Third Paragraph. Refer the reader to the enclosed résumé for more detailed information.

Fourth Paragraph. In this paragraph say what you will do to follow up on your letter. For example, state that you will call by a certain date to set up an interview or to find out if the company will be recruiting in your area. Finish by indicating your willingness to answer any questions the recipient may have. Be sure you have provided your phone number.

Sincerely,

Type your name

Enclosure

Exhibit 2.4
SAMPLE COVER LETTER

1145 Westin Drive
Salisbury, NC 28144
(704) 555-8167
cindyeast222@xxx.com

August 12, 2007

Ms. Roberta Keyes
Executive Vice President
Colonial America Foundation
2050 DuPont Circle
Washington, DC 20002

Dear Ms. Keyes:

Please accept the enclosed résumé and letters of recommendation in application for the position of program officer manager at your organization. This is in response to the job vacancy notice published this week in the *Chronicle of Philanthropy*.

As you will gather from my résumé, I have a solid knowledge of American history through my studies at Catawba College and Duke University, as well as my experiences working for the U.S. Park Service. In addition, my two years of experience with the North Carolina Historical Society as a grants management assistant has entailed responsibilities that are very similar to human resource management. In fact, I believe that my professional and educational background provides the ideal qualifications you are seeking.

I have always had a strong interest not only in history but also in philanthropy, and would enjoy the opportunity to apply my experience to the challenges of an organization such as yours.

I would appreciate an interview at your convenience. My telephone number is (704) 555-8167, and I can be reached there at any time through my voice-mail service.

Thank you for your consideration. I look forward to your response.

Sincerely,

Cindy East

Enclosure

3

Researching Careers and Networking

What do they call the job you want? One reason for confusion is perhaps a mistaken assumption that a college education provides job training. In most cases it does not. Of course, applied fields such as engineering, management, or education provide specific skills for the workplace as well as an education. Regardless, your overall college education exposes you to numerous fields of study and teaches you quantitative reasoning, critical thinking, writing, and speaking, all of which can be successfully applied to a number of different job fields. But it still remains up to you to choose a job field and to learn how to articulate the benefits of your education in a way the employer will appreciate.

One common question a career counselor encounters is "What can I do with my degree?" While some history majors have narrowed down their interests a little more successfully than others, the choices are not always clearly defined. History is a wide field, populated with scores of job titles you might never have heard of before. You know that history majors can go into museum work, teaching and research, or information management, to name just the major paths. However, you may still be confused as to exactly what kinds of jobs you can do with your degree, what your duties will be, and what kinds of organizations will hire you. Where does a history major fit into an information management firm? What does a history major actually do for a natural history museum?

Collect Job Titles

The world of employment is a complex place, so you need to become a bit of an explorer and adventurer and be willing to try a variety of techniques to develop a list of possible occupations that might use your talents and education. You might find computerized interest inventories, reference books and other sources, and classified ads helpful in this respect. Once you have a list of possibilities that you are interested in and qualified for, you can move on to find out what kinds of organizations have these job titles.

Computerized Interest Inventories

One way to begin collecting job titles is to identify a number of jobs that call for your degree and the particular skills and interests you identified as part of the self-assessment process. There are excellent interactive career-guidance programs on the market to help you produce such selected lists of possible job titles. Most of these are available at colleges and at some larger town and city libraries. Two of the industry leaders are CHOICES and DIS-COVER. Both allow you to enter interests, values, educational background, and other information to produce lists of possible occupations and industries. Each of the resources listed here will produce different job title lists. Some job titles will appear again and again, while others will be unique to a particular source. Investigate all of them!

Reference Sources

Books on the market that may be available through your local library or career counseling office also suggest various occupations related to specific majors. The following are only a few of the many good books on the market: *The College Board Guide to 150 Popular College Majors* and *College Majors and Careers: A Resource Guide for Effective Life Planning* both by Paul Phifer, and *Kaplan's What to Study: 101 Fields in a Flash*. All of these books list possible job titles within the academic major.

It's important to realize that not every employer seeking to hire someone with a history degree may be equally desirable to you. Some employment environments may be more attractive to you than others. A history major considering a career in education might pursue that option as a high school teacher, community college professor, professor at a four-year college or university, or in some nontraditional role such as a guide at a national historical park. Though these jobs might involve similar skills, each environment presents a different "culture" with associated norms in the pace of work, the interaction with others, and the background and training of those you'll work with or encounter on the job. Even in roles where job titles are quite similar, not all situations will present the same "fit" for you.

If you majored in history and enjoyed the in-class presentations you did as part of your degree and have developed some strong communication skills, you might naturally think of a teaching career. But history majors with these same skills and interests go on to work as nonprofit program officers, attorneys (after completing law school), and business executives, among other roles. Each job title in this list can be found in a variety of settings.

Each job title deserves your consideration. Like removing the layers of an onion, the search for job titles can go on and on! As you spend time doing this activity, you are actually learning more about the value of your degree. What's important in your search at this point is not to become critical or selective but rather to develop as long a list of possibilities as you can. Every source used will help you add new and potentially exciting jobs to your growing list.

Classified Ads

It has been well publicized that the classified ad section of the newspaper represents only a small fraction of the current job market. Nevertheless, the weekly classified ads can be a great help to you in your search. Although they may not be the best place to look for a job, they can teach you a lot about the job market. Classified ads provide a good education in job descriptions, duties, responsibilities, and qualifications. In addition, they provide insight into which industries are actively recruiting and some indication of the area's employment market. This is particularly helpful when seeking a position in a specific geographic area and/or a specific field. For your purposes, classified ads are a good source for job titles to add to your list.

Read the Sunday classified ads in a major market newspaper for several weeks in a row. Cut and paste all the ads that interest you and seem to call for something close to your education, skills, experience, and interests. Remember that classified ads are written for what an organization *hopes* to find; you don't have to meet absolutely every criterion. However, if certain requirements are stated as absolute minimums and you cannot meet them, it's best not to waste your time and that of the employer.

The weekly classified want ads exercise is important because these jobs are out in the marketplace. They truly exist, and people with your qualifications are being sought to apply. What's more, many of these advertisements describe the duties and responsibilities of the job advertised and give you a beginning sense of the challenges and opportunities such a position presents. Some will indicate salary, and that will be helpful as well. This information will better define the jobs for you and provide some good material for possible interviews in that field.

Explore Job Descriptions

Once you've arrived at a solid list of possible job titles that interest you and for which you believe you are somewhat qualified, it's a good idea to do some research on each of these jobs. The preeminent source for such job information is the Dictionary of Occupational Titles, or DOT (wave.net/upg/immigration/dot_index.html). This directory lists every conceivable job and provides excellent up-to-date information on duties and responsibilities, interactions with associates, and day-to-day assignments and tasks. These descriptions provide a thorough job analysis, but they do not consider the possible employers or the environments in which a job may be performed. So, although a position as public relations officer may be well defined in terms of duties and responsibilities, it does not explain the differences in doing public relations work in a college or a hospital or a factory or a bank. You will need to look somewhere else for work settings.

Learn More About Possible Work Settings

After reading some job descriptions, you may choose to edit and revise your list of job titles once again, discarding those you feel are not suitable and keeping those that continue to hold your interest. Or you may wish to keep your list intact and see where these jobs may be located. For example, if you are interested in public relations and you appear to have those skills and the requisite education, you'll want to know which organizations do public relations. How can you find that out? How much income does someone in public relations make a year and what is the employment potential for the field of public relations?

To answer these and many other questions about your list of job titles, we recommend you try any of the following resources: *Careers Encyclopedia*, the professional societies and resources found throughout this book, *College to Career: The Guide to Job Opportunities*, and the *Occupational Outlook Handbook* (http://stats.bls.gov/ocohome.htm). Each of these resources, in a different way, will help to put the job titles you have selected into an employer context. Perhaps the most extensive discussion is found in the *Occupational Outlook Handbook*, which gives a thorough presentation of the nature of the work, the working conditions, employment statistics, training, other qualifications, and advancement possibilities as well as job outlook and earnings. Related occupations are also detailed, and a select bibliography is provided to help you find additional information.

Continuing with our public relations example, your search through these reference materials would teach you that the public relations jobs you find attractive are available in larger hospitals, financial institutions, most corporations (both consumer goods and industrial goods), media organizations, and colleges and universities.

Networking

Networking is the process of deliberately establishing relationships to get career-related information or to alert potential employers that you are available for work. Networking is critically important to today's job seeker for two reasons: it will help you get the information you need, and it can help you find out about *all* of the available jobs.

Get the Information You Need

Networkers will review your résumé and give you feedback on its effectiveness. They will talk about the job you are looking for and give you a candid appraisal of how they see your strengths and weaknesses. If they have a good sense of the industry or the employment sector for that job, you'll get their feelings on future trends in the industry as well. Some networkers will be very forthcoming about salaries, job-hunting techniques, and suggestions for your job search strategy. Many have been known to place calls right from the interview desk to friends and associates who might be interested in you. Each networker will make his or her own contribution, and each will be valuable.

Because organizations must evolve to adapt to current global market needs, the information provided by decision makers within various organizations will be critical to your success as a new job market entrant. For example, you might learn about the concept of virtual organizations from a networker. Virtual organizations coordinate economic activity to deliver value to customers by using resources outside the traditional boundaries of the organization. This concept is being discussed and implemented by chief executive officers of many organizations, including Ford Motor, Dell, and IBM. Networking can help you find out about this and other trends currently affecting the industries under your consideration.

Find Out About All of the Available Jobs

Not every job that is available at this very moment is advertised for potential applicants to see. This is called the *hidden job market*. Only 15 to 20 percent of all jobs are formally advertised, which means that 80 to 85 percent of available jobs do not appear in published channels. Networking will help you become more knowledgeable about all the employment opportunities available during your job search period.

Although someone you might talk to today doesn't know of any openings within his or her organization, tomorrow or next week or next month an opening may occur. If you've taken the time to show an interest in and knowledge of their organization, if you've shown the company representative how you can help achieve organizational goals and that you can fit into the organization, you'll be one of the first candidates considered for the position.

Networking: A Proactive Approach

Networking is a proactive rather than a reactive approach. You, as a job seeker, are expected to initiate a certain level of activity on your own behalf; you cannot afford to simply respond to jobs listed in the newspaper. Being proactive means building a network of contacts that includes informed and interested decision makers who will provide you with up-to-date knowledge of the current job market and increase your chances of finding out about employment opportunities appropriate for your interests, experience, and level of education. An old axiom of networking says, "You are only two phone calls away from the information you need." In other words, by talking to enough people, you will quickly come across someone who can offer you help.

Preparing to Network

In deliberately establishing relationships, maximize your efforts by organizing your approach. Five specific areas in which you can organize your efforts include reviewing your self-assessment, reviewing your research on job sites and organizations, deciding who you want to talk to, keeping track of all your efforts, and creating your self-promotion tools.

Review Your Self-Assessment

Your self-assessment is as important a tool in preparing to network as it has been in other aspects of your job search. You have carefully evaluated your personal traits, personal values, economic needs, longer-term goals, skill base, preferred skills, and underdeveloped skills. During the networking process you will be called upon to communicate what you know about yourself and relate it to the information or job you seek. Be sure to review the exercises that you completed in the self-assessment section of this book in preparation for networking. We've explained that you need to assess which skills you have acquired from your major that are of general value to an employer; be ready to express those in ways he or she can appreciate as useful in the organizations.

Review Research on Job Sites and Organizations

In addition, individuals assisting you will expect that you'll have at least some background information on the occupation or industry of interest to you. Refer to the appropriate sections of this book and other relevant publications to acquire the background information necessary for effective networking. They'll explain how to identify not only the job titles that might be of interest to you but also which kinds of organizations employ people to do that job. You will develop some sense of working conditions and expectations about duties and responsibilities—all of which will be of help in your networking interviews.

Decide Whom You Want to Talk To

Networking cannot begin until you decide who you want to talk to and, in general, what type of information you hope to gain from your contacts. Once you know this, it's time to begin developing a list of contacts. Five useful sources for locating contacts are described here.

College Alumni Network. Most colleges and universities have created a formal network of alumni and friends of the institution who are particularly interested in helping currently enrolled students and graduates of their alma mater gain employment-related information.

It is usually a simple process to make use of an alumni network. Visit your college's website and locate the alumni office and/or your career center. Either or both sites will have information about your school's alumni network. You'll be provided with information on shadowing experiences, geographic information, or those alumni offering job referrals. If you don't find what you're looking for, don't hesitate to phone or e-mail your career center and ask what they can do to help you connect with an alum.

Alumni networkers may provide some combination of the following services: day-long shadowing experiences, telephone interviews, in-person interviews, information on relocating to given geographic areas, internship information, suggestions on graduate school study, and job vacancy notices.

Present and Former Supervisors. If you believe you are on good terms with present or former job supervisors, they may be an excellent resource for providing information or directing you to appropriate resources that would have information related to your current interests and needs. Additionally, these supervisors probably belong to professional organizations that they might be willing to utilize to get information for you.

Employers in Your Area. Although you may be interested in working in a geographic location different from the one where you currently reside, don't overlook the value of the knowledge and contacts those around you are able to provide. Use the local telephone directory and newspaper to identify the types of organizations you are thinking of working for or professionals who have the kinds of jobs you are interested in. Recently, a call made to a local hospital's financial administrator for information on working in health-care financial administration yielded more pertinent information on training seminars, regional professional organizations, and potential employment sites than a national organization was willing to provide.

Employers in Geographic Areas Where You Hope to Work. If you are thinking about relocating, identifying prospective employers or informational contacts in the new location will be critical to your success. Here are some tips for online searching. First, use a "metasearch" engine to get the most out of your search. Metasearch engines combine several engines into one powerful tool. We frequently use dogpile.com and metasearch.com for this purpose. Try using the city and state as your keywords in a search. *New Haven, Connecticut* will bring you to the city's website with links to the chamber of commerce, member businesses, and other valuable resources. By using looksmart.com you can locate newspapers in any area, and they, too, can provide valuable insight before you relocate. Of course, both dogpile and metasearch can lead you to yellow and white page directories in areas you are considering.

Professional Associations and Organizations. Professional associations and organizations can provide valuable information in several areas: career paths that you might not have considered, qualifications relating to those career choices, publications that list current job openings, and workshops or seminars that will enhance your professional knowledge and skills. They can also be excellent sources for background information on given industries: their health, current problems, and future challenges.

There are several excellent resources available to help you locate professional associations and organizations that would have information to meet your needs. Two especially useful publications are the *Encyclopedia of Associations* and *National Trade and Professional Associations of the United States*.

Keep Track of All Your Efforts

It can be difficult, almost impossible, to remember all the details related to each contact you make during the networking process, so you will want to develop a record-keeping system that works for you. Formalize this process by using your computer to keep a record of the people and organizations you want to contact. You can simply record the contact's name, address, and telephone number, and what information you hope to gain.

You could record this as a simple Word document and you could still use the "Find" function if you were trying to locate some data and could only recall the firm's name or the contact's name. If you're comfortable with database management and you have some database software on your computer, then you can put information at your fingertips even if you have only the zip code! The point here is not technological sophistication but good record keeping.

Once you have created this initial list, it will be helpful to keep more detailed information as you begin to actually make the contacts. Those details should include complete contact information, the date and content of each contact, names and information for additional networkers, and required follow-up. Don't forget to send a letter thanking your contact for his or her time! Your contact will appreciate your recall of details of your meetings and conversations, and the information will help you to focus your networking efforts.

Create Your Self-Promotion Tools

There are two types of promotional tools that are used in the networking process. The first is a résumé and cover letter, and the second is a one-minute "infomercial," which may be given over the telephone or in person.

Techniques for writing an effective résumé and cover letter are discussed in Chapter 2. Once you have reviewed that material and prepared these important documents, you will have created one of your self-promotion tools.

The one-minute infomercial will demand that you begin tying your interests, abilities, and skills to the people or organizations you want to network with. Think about your goal for making the contact to help you understand what you should say about yourself. You should be able to express yourself easily and convincingly. If, for example, you are contacting an alumnus of your institution to obtain the names of possible employment sites in a distant city, be prepared to discuss why you are interested in moving to that location, the types of jobs you are interested in, and the skills and abilities you possess that will make you a qualified candidate.

To create a meaningful one-minute infomercial, write it out, practice it as if it will be a spoken presentation, rewrite it, and practice it again if necessary until expressing yourself comes easily and is convincing.

Here's a simplified example of an infomercial for use over the telephone:

Hello, Mr. Chen? My name is Roger Wagner. I am a recent graduate of Concord University, and I wish to enter the nonprofit field. I feel confident I have many of the skills I understand are valued for managers in nonprofit settings. Along with a degree in history, I have a strong quantitative background, with good research and computer skills. In addition, I have excellent interpersonal skills and am known as a compassionate, caring individual. I understand these are valuable traits in your line of work.

Mr. Chen, I'm calling you because I still need more information about nonprofit management and where I might fit in. I'm hoping you'll have time to sit down with me for about half an hour and discuss your perspective on careers. There are so many possible employers to approach, and I am seeking some advice on which might be the best bet for my particular combination of skills and experience.

Would you be willing to do that for me? I would greatly appreciate it. I am available most mornings, if that's convenient for you.

It very well may happen that your employer contact wishes you to communicate by e-mail. The infomercial quoted above could easily be rewritten for an e-mail message. You should "cut and paste" your résumé right into the e-mail text itself.

Other effective self-promotion tools include portfolios for those in the arts, writing professions, or teaching. Portfolios show examples of work, photographs of projects or classroom activities, or certificates and credentials that are job related. There may not be an opportunity to use the portfolio during an interview, and it is not something that should be left with the organization. It is designed to be explained and displayed by the creator. However, during some networking meetings, there may be an opportunity to illustrate a point or strengthen a qualification by exhibiting the portfolio.

Beginning the Networking Process

Set the Tone for Your Communications

It can be useful to establish "tone words" for any communications you embark upon. Before making your first telephone call or writing your first letter, decide what you want the person to think of you. If you are networking to try to obtain a job, your tone words might include descriptors such as *genuine*, *informed*, and *self-knowledgeable*. When you're trying to acquire information, your tone words may have a slightly different focus, such as *courteous*, *organized*, *focused*, and *well-spoken*. Use the tone words you establish for your contacts to guide you through the networking process.

Honestly Express Your Intentions

When contacting individuals, it is important to be honest about your reasons for making the contact. Establish your purpose in your own mind and be able and ready to articulate it concisely. Determine an initial agenda, whether it be informational questioning or self-promotion, present it to your contact, and be ready to respond immediately. If you don't adequately prepare before initiating your overture, you may find yourself at a disadvantage if you're asked to immediately begin your informational interview or self-promotion during the first phone conversation or visit.

Start Networking Within Your Circle of Confidence

Once you have organized your approach—by utilizing specific researching methods, creating a system for keeping track of the people you will contact, and developing effective self-promotion tools—you are ready to begin networking. The best way to begin networking is by talking with a group of people you trust and feel comfortable with. This group is usually made up of your family, friends, and career counselors. No matter who is in this inner circle, they will have a special interest in seeing you succeed in your job search. In addition, because they will be easy to talk to, you should try taking some risks in terms of practicing your information-seeking approach. Gain confidence in talking about the strengths you bring to an organization and the underdeveloped skills you feel hinder your candidacy. Be sure to review the section on self-assessment for tips on approaching each of these areas. Ask for critical but constructive feedback from the people in your circle of confidence on the letters you write and the one-minute infomercial you have developed. Evaluate whether you want to make the changes they suggest, then practice the changes on others within this circle.

Stretch the Boundaries of Your Networking Circle of Confidence

Once you have refined the promotional tools you will use to accomplish your networking goals, you will want to make additional contacts. Because you will not know most of these people, it will be a less comfortable activity to undertake. The practice that you gained with your inner circle of trusted friends should have prepared you to now move outside of that comfort zone.

It is said that any information a person needs is only two phone calls away, but the information cannot be gained until you (1) make a reasonable guess about who might have the information you need and (2) pick up the telephone to make the call. Using your network list that includes alumni, instructors, supervisors, employers, and associations, you can begin preparing your list of questions that will allow you to get the information you need.

Prepare the Questions You Want to Ask

Networkers can provide you with the insider's perspective on any given field and you can ask them questions that you might not want to ask in an interview. For example, you can ask them to describe the more repetitious or mundane parts of the job or ask them for a realistic idea of salary expectations. Be sure to prepare your questions ahead of time so that you are organized and efficient.

Be Prepared to Answer Some Questions

To communicate effectively, you must anticipate questions that will be asked of you by the networkers you contact. Revisit the self-assessment process you undertook and the research you've done so that you can effortlessly respond to questions about your short- and long-term goals and the kinds of jobs you are most interested in pursuing.

General Networking Tips

Make Every Contact Count. Setting the tone for each interaction is critical. Approaches that will help you communicate in an effective way include politeness, being appreciative of time provided to you, and being prepared and thorough. Remember, *everyone* within an organization has a circle of influence, so be prepared to interact effectively with each person you encounter in the networking process, including secretarial and support staff. Many information or job seekers have thwarted their own efforts by being rude to some individuals they encountered as they networked because they made the incorrect assumption that certain persons were unimportant.

Sometimes your contacts may be surprised at their ability to help you. After meeting and talking with you, they might think they have not offered much in the way of help. A day or two later, however, they may make a contact that would be useful to you and refer you to that person.

With Each Contact, Widen Your Circle of Networkers. Always leave an informational interview with the names of at least two more people who can help you get the information or job that you are seeking. Don't be shy about asking for additional contacts; networking is all about increasing the number of people you can interact with to achieve your goals.

Make Your Own Decisions. As you talk with different people and get answers to the questions you pose, you may hear conflicting information or get conflicting suggestions. Your job is to listen to these "experts" and decide what information and which suggestions will help you achieve *your* goals. Only implement those suggestions that you believe will work for you.

Shutting Down Your Network

As you achieve the goals that motivated your networking activity—getting the information you need or the job you want—the time will come to inactivate all or parts of your network. As you do, be sure to tell your primary supporters about your change in status. Call or write to each one of them and give them as many details about your new status as you feel is necessary to maintain a positive relationship.

Because a network takes on a life of its own, activity undertaken on your behalf will continue even after you cease your efforts. As you get calls or are contacted in some fashion, be sure to inform these networkers about your change in status, and thank them for assistance they have provided.

Information on the latest employment trends indicates that workers will change jobs or careers several times in their lifetime. Networking, then, will be a critical aspect in the span of your professional life. If you carefully and thoughtfully conduct your networking activities during your job search, you will have a solid foundation of experience when you need to network the next time around.

Where Are These Jobs, Anyway?

Having a list of job titles that you've designed around your own career interests and skills is an excellent beginning. It means you've really thought about who you are and what you are presenting to the employment market. It has caused you to think seriously about the most appealing environments to work in, and you have identified some employer types that represent these environments.

The research and the thinking that you've done thus far will be used again and again. They will be helpful in writing your résumé and cover letters, in talking about yourself on the telephone to prospective employers, and in answering interview questions.

Now is a good time to begin to narrow the field of job titles and employment sites down to some specific employers to initiate the employment contact.

Find Out Which Employers Hire People Like You

This section will provide tips, techniques, and specific resources for developing an actual list of specific employers that can be used to make contacts. It is only an outline that you must be prepared to tailor to your own particular needs and according to what you bring to the job search. Once again, it is important to communicate with others along the way exactly what you're looking for and what your goals are for the research you're doing. Librarians, employers, career counselors, friends, friends of friends, business contacts, and bookstore staff will all have helpful information on geographically specific and new resources to aid you in locating employers who'll hire you.

Identify Information Resources

Your interview wardrobe and your new résumé might have put a dent in your wallet, but the resources you'll need to pursue your job search are available for free. The categories of information detailed here are not hard to find and are yours for the browsing.

Numerous resources described in this section will help you identify actual employers. Use all of them or any others that you identify as available in your geographic area. As you become experienced in this process, you'll quickly figure out which information sources are helpful and which are not. If you live in a rural area, a well-planned day trip to a major city that includes a college career office, a large college or city library, state and federal employment centers, a chamber of commerce office, and a well-stocked bookstore can produce valuable results.

There are many excellent resources available to help you identify actual job sites. They are categorized into employer directories (usually indexed by product lines and geographic location), geographically based directories (designed to highlight particular cities, regions, or states), career-specific directories (e.g., *Sports MarketPlace*, which lists tens of thousands of firms involved with sports), periodicals and newspapers, targeted job posting publications, and videos. This is by no means meant to be a complete treatment of resources but rather a starting point for identifying useful resources.

Working from the more general references to highly specific resources, we provide a basic list to help you begin your search. Many of these you'll find easily available. In some cases reference librarians and others will suggest even better materials for your particular situation. Start to create your own customized bibliography of job search references.

Geographically Based Directories. The Job Bank series published by Bob Adams, Inc. (aip.com) contains detailed entries on each area's major employers, including business activity, address, phone number, and hiring contact name. Many listings specify educational backgrounds being sought in potential employees. Each volume contains a solid discussion of each city's or state's major employment sectors. Organizations are also indexed by industry. Job Bank volumes are available for the following places: Atlanta, Boston, Chicago, Dallas–Ft. Worth, Denver, Detroit, Florida, Houston, Los Angeles, Minneapolis, New York, Ohio, Philadelphia, San Francisco, Seattle, St. Louis, Washington, D.C., and other cities throughout the Northwest.

National Job Bank (careercity.com) lists employers in every state, along with contact names and commonly hired job categories. Included are many small companies often overlooked by other directories. Companies are also indexed by industry. This publication provides information on educational backgrounds sought and lists company benefits.

Periodicals and Newspapers. Several sources are available to help you locate which journals or magazines carry job advertisements in your field. Other resources help you identify opportunities in other parts of the country.

- *Where the Jobs Are: A Comprehensive Directory of 1200 Journals Listing Career Opportunities*
- *Corptech Fast 5000 Company Locator*
- *National Ad Search* (nationaladsearch.com)
- *The Federal Jobs Digest* (jobsfed.com) and *Federal Career Opportunities*
- *World Chamber of Commerce Directory* (chamberofcommerce.org)

This list is certainly not exhaustive; use it to begin your job search work.

Targeted Job Posting Publications. Although the resources that follow are national in scope, they are either targeted to one medium of contact (telephone), focused on specific types of jobs, or less comprehensive than the sources previously listed.

- Careers.org (careers.org/index.html)
- *The Job Hunter* (jobhunter.com)
- *Current Jobs for Graduates* (graduatejobs.com)
- *Environmental Opportunities* (ecojobs.com)
- *Y National Vacancy List* (ymca.net/employment/ymca_recruiting/jobright.htm)
- *ArtSEARCH*
- *Community Jobs*
- *National Association of Colleges and Employers: Job Choices series*
- *National Association of Colleges and Employers* (jobweb.com)

Videos. You may be one of the many job seekers who likes to get information via a medium other than paper. Many career libraries, public libraries, and career centers in libraries carry an assortment of videos that will help you learn new techniques and get information helpful in the job search.

Locate Information Resources
Throughout these introductory chapters, we have continually referred you to various websites for information on everything from job listings to career information. Using the Web gives you a mobility at your computer that you don't enjoy if you rely solely on books or newspapers or printed journals. Moreover, material on the Web, if the site is maintained, can be the most up-to-date information available.

You'll eventually identify the information resources that work best for you, but make certain you've covered the full range of resources before you begin to rely on a smaller list. Here's a short list of informational sites that many job seekers find helpful:

- Public and college libraries
- College career centers
- Bookstores
- The Internet
- Local and state government personnel offices
- Career/job fairs

Each one of these sites offers a collection of resources that will help you get the information you need.

As you meet and talk with service professionals at all these sites, be sure to let them know what you're doing. Inform them of your job search, what you've already accomplished, and what you're looking for. The more people who know you're job seeking, the greater the possibility that someone will have information or know someone who can help you along your way.

4

Interviewing and Job Offer Considerations

Certainly, there can be no one part of the job search process more fraught with anxiety and worry than the interview. Yet seasoned job seekers welcome the interview and will often say, "Just get me an interview and I'm on my way!" They understand that the interview is crucial to the hiring process and equally crucial for them, as job candidates, to have the opportunity of a personal dialogue to add to what the employer may already have learned from the résumé, cover letter, and telephone conversations.

Believe it or not, the interview is to be welcomed, and even enjoyed! It is a perfect opportunity for you, the candidate, to sit down with an employer and express yourself and display who you are and what you want. Of course, it takes thought and planning and a little strategy; after all, it *is* a job interview! But it can be a positive, if not pleasant, experience and one you can look back on and feel confident about your performance and effort.

For many new job seekers, a job, any job, seems a wonderful thing. But seasoned interview veterans know that the job interview is an important step for both sides—the employer and the candidate—to see what each has to offer and whether there is going to be a "fit" of personalities, work styles, and attitudes. And it is this concept of balance in the interview, that both sides have important parts to play, that holds the key to success in mastering this aspect of the job search strategy.

Try to think of the interview as a conversation between two interested and equal partners. You both have important, even vital, information to deliver and to learn. Of course, there's no denying the employer has some leverage, especially in the initial interview for recruitment or any interview scheduled by the candidate and not the recruiter. That should not prevent the interviewee from seeking to play an equal part in what should be a fair exchange of information. Too often the untutored candidate allows the interview to become one-sided. The employer asks all the questions and the candidate simply responds. The ideal would be for two mutually interested parties to sit down and discuss possibilities for each. This is a conversation of significance, and it requires preparation, thought about the tone of the interview, and planning of the nature and details of the information to be exchanged.

Preparing for the Interview

The length of most initial interviews is about thirty minutes. Given the brevity, the information that is exchanged ought to be important. The candidate should be delivering material that the employer cannot discover on the résumé, and in turn, the candidate should be learning things about the employer that he or she could not otherwise find out. After all, if you have only thirty minutes, why waste time on information that is already published? The information exchanged is more than just factual, and both sides will learn much from what they see of each other, as well. How the candidate looks, speaks, and acts are important to the employer. The employer's attention to the interview and awareness of the candidate's résumé, the setting, and the quality of information presented are important to the candidate.

Just as the employer has every right to be disappointed when a prospect is late for the interview, looks unkempt, and seems ill-prepared to answer fairly standard questions, the candidate may be disappointed with an interviewer who isn't ready for the meeting, hasn't learned the basic résumé facts, and is constantly interrupted by telephone calls. In either situation there's good reason to feel let down.

There are many elements to a successful interview, and some of them are not easy to describe or prepare for. Sometimes there is just a chemistry between interviewer and interviewee that brings out the best in both, and a good exchange takes place. But there is much the candidate can do to pave the way for success in terms of his or her résumé, personal appearance, goals, and interview strategy—each of which we will discuss. However, none of this preparation is as important as the time and thought the candidate gives to personal self-assessment.

Self-Assessment

Neither a stunning résumé nor an expensive, well-tailored suit can compensate for candidates who do not know what they want, where they are going, or why they are interviewing with a particular employer. Self-assessment, the process by which we begin to know and acknowledge our own particular blend of education, experiences, needs, and goals, is not something that can be sorted out the weekend before a major interview. Of all the elements of interview preparation, this one requires the longest lead time and cannot be faked.

Because the time allotted for most interviews is brief, it is all the more important for job candidates to understand and express succinctly why they are there and what they have to offer. This is not a time for undue modesty (or for braggadocio either); it is a time for a compelling, reasoned statement of why you feel that you and this employer might make a good match. It means you have to have thought about your skills, interests, and attributes; related those to your life experiences and your own history of challenges and opportunities; and determined what that indicates about your strengths, preferences, values, and areas needing further development.

If you need some assistance with self-assessment issues, refer to Chapter 1. Included are suggested exercises that can be done as needed, such as making up an experiential diary and extracting obvious strengths and weaknesses from past experiences. These simple assignments will help you look at past activities as collections of tasks with accompanying skills and responsibilities. Don't overlook your high school or college career office. Many offer personal counseling on self-assessment issues and may provide testing instruments such as the *Myers-Briggs Type Indicator (MBTI)*, the *Harrington-O'Shea Career Decision-Making System (CDM)*, the *Strong Interest Inventory (SII)*, or any other of a wide selection of assessment tools that can help you clarify some of these issues prior to the interview stage of your job search.

The Résumé

Résumé preparation has been discussed in detail, and some basic examples were provided. In this section we want to concentrate on how best to use your résumé in the interview. In most cases the employer will have seen the résumé prior to the interview, and, in fact, it may well have been the quality of that résumé that secured the interview opportunity.

An interview is a conversation, however, and not an exercise in reading. So, if the employer hasn't seen your résumé and you have brought it along to the interview, wait until asked or until the end of the interview to offer it. Otherwise, you may find yourself staring at the back of your résumé and simply answering "yes" and "no" to a series of questions drawn from that document.

Sometimes an interviewer is not prepared and does not know or recall the contents of the résumé and may use the résumé to a greater or lesser degree as a "prompt" during the interview. It is for you to judge what that may indicate about the individual performing the interview or the employer. If your interviewer seems surprised by the scheduled meeting, relies on the résumé to an inordinate degree, and seems otherwise unfamiliar with your background, this lack of preparation for the hiring process could well be a symptom of general management disorganization or may simply be the result of poor planning on the part of one individual. It is your responsibility as a potential employee to be aware of these signals and make your decisions accordingly.

At any rate, it is entirely acceptable for you to bring the conversation back to a more interpersonal style by saying something like, "Ms. Lawson, you might be interested in some recent experience I gained in a volunteer position at our county historical society that is not reflected on my application. May I tell you about this experience?" This approach can change the interview from one person reading and another responding, to more of a conversation between two people.

By all means, bring at least one copy of your résumé to the interview. Occasionally, at the close of an interview, an interviewer will express an interest in circulating a résumé to several departments, and you could then offer the copy you brought. Sometimes, an interview appointment provides an opportunity to meet others in the organization who may express an interest in you and your background, and it may be helpful to follow up with a copy of your résumé. Our best advice, however, is to keep it out of sight until needed or requested.

Employer Information

Whether your interview is for graduate school admission, an overseas corporate position, or a position with a local company, it is important to know something about the employer or the organization. Keeping in mind that the interview is relatively brief and that you will hopefully have other interviews with other organizations, it is important to keep your research in proportion. If secondary interviews are called for, you will have additional time to do further research. For the first interview, it is helpful to know the organization's mission, goals, size, scope of operations, and so forth. Your research may uncover recent areas of challenge or particular successes that may help to fuel the interview. Use the "What Do They Call the Job You Want?"

section of Chapter 3, your library, and your career or guidance office to help you locate this information in the most efficient way possible. Don't be shy in asking advice of these counseling and guidance professionals on how best to spend your preparation time. With some practice, you'll soon learn how much information is enough and which kinds of information are most useful to you.

Interview Content

We've already discussed how it can help to think of the interview as an important conversation—one that, as with any conversation, you want to find pleasant and interesting and to leave you with a good feeling. But because this conversation is especially important, the information that's exchanged is critical to its success. What do you want them to know about you? What do you need to know about them? What interview technique do you need to particularly pay attention to? How do you want to manage the close of the interview? What steps will follow in the hiring process?

Except for the professional interviewer, most of us find interviewing stressful and anxiety-provoking. Developing a strategy before you begin interviewing will help you relieve some stress and anxiety. One particular strategy that has worked for many and may work for you is interviewing by objective. Before you interview, write down three to five goals you would like to achieve for that interview. They may be technique goals: smile a little more, have a firmer handshake, be sure to ask about the next stage in the interview process before leaving. They may be content-oriented goals: find out about the company's current challenges and opportunities; be sure to speak of your recent research, writing experiences, or foreign travel. Whatever your goals, jot down a few of them as goals for each interview.

Most people find that in trying to achieve these few goals, their interviewing technique becomes more organized and focused. After the interview, the most common question friends and family ask is "How did it go?" With this technique, you have an indication of whether you met *your* goals for the meeting, not just some vague idea of how it went. Chances are, if you accomplished what you wanted to, it improved the quality of the entire interview. As you continue to interview, you will want to revise your goals to continue improving your interview skills.

Now, add to the concept of the significant conversation the idea of a beginning, a middle, and a closing and you will have two thoughts that will give your interview a distinctive character. Be sure to make your introduction warm and cordial. Say your full name (and if it's a difficult-to-pronounce name, help the interviewer to pronounce it) and make certain you know your interviewer's name and how to pronounce it. Most interviews begin with some "soft talk" about the weather, chat about the candidate's trip to the interview site, or national events. This is done as a courtesy to relax both you and the interviewer, to get you talking, and to generally try to defuse the atmosphere of excessive tension. Try to be yourself, engage in the conversation, and don't try to second-guess the interviewer. This is simply what it appears to be—casual conversation.

Once you and the interviewer move on to exchange more serious information in the middle part of the interview, the two most important concerns become your ability to handle challenging questions and your success at asking meaningful ones. Interviewer questions will probably fall into one of three categories: personal assessment and career direction, academic assessment, and knowledge of the employer. Here are a few examples of questions in each category:

Personal Assessment and Career Direction
1. What motivates you to put forth your best effort?
2. What do you consider to be your greatest strengths and weaknesses?
3. What qualifications do you have that make you think you will be successful in this career?

Academic Assessment
1. What led you to choose your major?
2. What subjects did you like best and least? Why?
3. How has your college experience prepared you for this career?

Knowledge of the Employer
1. What do you think it takes to be successful in an organization like ours?
2. In what ways do you think you can make a contribution to our organization?
3. Why did you choose to seek a position with this organization?

The interviewer wants a response to each question but is also gauging your enthusiasm, preparedness, and willingness to communicate. In each response you should provide some information about yourself that can be related to the employer's needs. A common mistake is to give too much information. Answer each question completely, but be careful not to run on too long with extensive details or examples.

Questions About Underdeveloped Skills

Most employers interview people who have met some minimum criteria of education and experience. They interview candidates to see who they are, to learn what kind of personality they exhibit, and to get some sense of how they might fit into the existing organization. It may be that you are asked about skills the employer hopes to find and that you have not documented. Maybe it's grant-writing experience, knowledge of the European political system, or a knowledge of the film world.

To questions about skills and experiences you don't have, answer honestly and forthrightly and try to offer some additional information about skills you do have. For example, perhaps the employer is disappointed you have no grant-writing experience. An honest answer may be as follows:

> *No, unfortunately, I was never in a position to acquire those skills. I do understand something of the complexities of the grant-writing process and feel confident that my attention to detail, careful reading skills, and strong writing would make grants a wonderful challenge in a new job. I think I could get up on the learning curve quickly.*

The employer hears an honest admission of lack of experience but is reassured by some specific skill details that do relate to grant writing and a confident manner that suggests enthusiasm and interest in a challenge.

For many students, questions about their possible contribution to an employer's organization can prove challenging. Because your education has probably not included specific training for a job, you need to review your academic record and select capabilities you have developed in your major that an employer can appreciate. For example, perhaps you read well and can analyze and condense what you've read into smaller, more focused pieces. That could be valuable. Or maybe you did some serious research and you know you have valuable investigative skills. Your public speaking might be highly developed and you might use visual aids appropriately and effectively. Or maybe your skill at correspondence, memos, and messages is effective. Whatever it is, you must take it out of the academic context and put it into a new, employer-friendly context so your interviewer can best judge how you could help the organization.

Exhibiting knowledge of the organization will, without a doubt, show the interviewer that you are interested enough in the available position to have done some legwork in preparation for the interview. Remember, it is not necessary to know every detail of the organization's history but rather to have a general knowledge about why it is in business and how the industry is faring.

Sometime during the interview, generally after the midway point, you'll be asked if you have any questions for the interviewer. Your questions will tell the employer much about your attitude and your desire to understand the organization's expectations so you can compare them to your own strengths. The following are just a few questions you might want to ask:

1. What is the communication style of the organization? (meetings, memos, and so forth)
2. What would a typical day in this position be like for me?
3. What have been some of the interesting challenges and opportunities your organization has recently faced?

Most interviews draw to a natural closing point, so be careful not to prolong the discussion. At a signal from the interviewer, wind up your presentation, express your appreciation for the opportunity, and be sure to ask what the next stage in the process will be. When can you expect to hear from them? Will they be conducting second-tier interviews? If you are interested and haven't heard, would they mind a phone call? Be sure to collect a business card with the name and phone number of your interviewer. On your way out, you might have an opportunity to pick up organizational literature you haven't seen before.

With the right preparation—a thorough self-assessment, professional clothing, and employer information—you'll be able to set and achieve the goals you have established for the interview process.

Interview Follow-Up

Quite often there is a considerable time lag between interviewing for a position and being hired or, in the case of the networker, between your phone call or letter to a possible contact and the opportunity of a meeting. This can be frustrating. "Why aren't they contacting me?" "I thought I'd get another interview, but no one has telephoned." "Am I out of the running?" You don't know what is happening.

Consider the Differing Perspectives
Of course, there is another perspective—that of the networker or hiring organization. Organizations are complex, with multiple tasks that need to be accomplished each day. Hiring is a discrete activity that does not occur as frequently as other job assignments. The hiring process might have to take

second place to other, more immediate organizational needs. Although it may be very important to you, and it is certainly ultimately significant to the employer, other issues such as fiscal management, planning and product development, employer vacation periods, or financial constraints may prevent an organization or individual within that organization from acting on your employment or your request for information as quickly as you or they would prefer.

Use Your Communications Skills

Good communication is essential here to resolve any anxieties, and the responsibility is on you, the job or information seeker. Too many job seekers and networkers offer as an excuse that they don't want to "bother" the organization by writing letters or calling. Let us assure you here and now, once and for all, that if you are troubling an organization by over-communicating, someone will indicate that situation to you quite clearly. If not, you can only assume you are a worthwhile prospect and the employer appreciates being reminded of your availability and interest. Let's look at follow-up practices in the job interview process and the networking situation separately.

Following Up on the Employment Interview

A brief thank-you note following an interview is an excellent and polite way to begin a series of follow-up communications with a potential employer with whom you have interviewed and want to remain in touch. It should be just that—a thank-you for a good meeting. If you failed to mention some fact or experience during your interview that you think might add to your candidacy, you may use this note to do that. However, this should be essentially a note whose overall tone is appreciative and, if appropriate, indicative of a continuing interest in pursuing any opportunity that may exist with that organization. It is one of the few pieces of business correspondence that may be handwritten, but always use plain, good-quality, standard-size paper.

If, however, at this point you are no longer interested in the employer, the thank-you note is an appropriate time to indicate that. You are under no obligation to identify any reason for not continuing to pursue employment with that organization, but if you are so inclined to indicate your professional reasons (pursuing other employers more akin to your interests, looking for greater income production than this employer can provide, a different geographic location), you certainly may. It should not be written with an eye to negotiation, for it will not be interpreted as such.

As part of your interview closing, you should have taken the initiative to establish lines of communication for continuing information about your candidacy. If you asked permission to telephone, wait a week following your thank-you note, then telephone your contact simply to inquire how things are progressing on your employment status. The feedback you receive here should be taken at face value. If your interviewer simply has no information, he or she will tell you so and indicate whether you should call again and when. Don't be discouraged if this should continue over some period of time.

If during this time something occurs that you think improves or changes your candidacy (some new qualification or experience you may have had), including any offers from other organizations, by all means telephone or write to inform the employer about this. In the case of an offer from a competing but less desirable or equally desirable organization, telephone your contact, explain what has happened, express your real interest in the organization, and inquire whether some determination on your employment might be made before you must respond to this other offer. An organization that is truly interested in you may be moved to make a decision about your candidacy. Equally possible is the scenario in which they are not yet ready to make a decision and so advise you to take the offer that has been presented. Again, you have no ethical alternative but to deal with the information presented in a straightforward manner.

When accepting other employment, be sure to contact any employers still actively considering you and inform them of your new job. Thank them graciously for their consideration. There are many other job seekers out there just like you who will benefit from having their candidacy improved when others bow out of the race. Who knows, you might at some future time have occasion to interact professionally with one of the organizations with which you sought employment. How embarrassing it would be to have someone remember you as the candidate who failed to notify them that you were taking a job elsewhere!

In all of your follow-up communications, keep good notes of whom you spoke with, when you called, and any instructions that were given about return communications. This will prevent any misunderstandings and provide you with good records of what has transpired.

Job Offer Considerations

For many recent college graduates, the thrill of their first job and, for some, the most substantial regular income they have ever earned seems an excess of good fortune coming at once. To question that first income or to be critical in any way of the conditions of employment at the time of the initial offer seems like looking a gift horse in the mouth. It doesn't seem to occur to many new hires even to attempt to negotiate any aspect of their first job. And, as many employers who deal with entry-level jobs for recent college graduates will readily confirm, the reality is that there simply isn't much movement in salary available to these new college recruits. The entry-level hire generally does not have an employment track record on a professional level to provide any leverage for negotiation. Real negotiations on salary, benefits, retirement provisions, and so forth come to those with significant employment records at higher income levels.

Of course, the job offer is more than just money. It can be composed of geographic assignment, duties and responsibilities, training, benefits, health and medical insurance, educational assistance, car allowance or company vehicle, and a host of other items. All of this is generally detailed in the formal letter that presents the final job offer. In most cases this is a follow-up to a personal phone call from the employer representative who has been principally responsible for your hiring process.

That initial telephone offer is certainly binding as a verbal agreement, but most firms follow up with a detailed letter outlining the most significant parts of your employment contract. You may, of course, choose to respond immediately at the time of the telephone offer (which would be considered a binding oral contract), but you will also be required to formally answer the letter of offer with a letter of acceptance, restating the salient elements of the . employer's description of your position, salary, and benefits. This ensures that both parties are clear on the terms and conditions of employment and remuneration and any other outstanding aspects of the job offer.

Is This the Job You Want?

Most new employees will respond affirmatively in writing, glad to be in the position to accept employment. If you've worked hard to get the offer and the job market is tight, other offers may not be in sight, so you will say, "Yes, I accept!" What is important here is that the job offer you accept be one that does fit your particular needs, values, and interests as you've outlined them in your self-assessment process. Moreover, it should be a job that will not only use your skills and education but also challenge you to develop new skills and talents.

Jobs are sometimes accepted too hastily, for the wrong reasons, and without proper scrutiny by the applicant. For example, an individual might readily accept a sales job only to find the continual rejection by potential clients unendurable. An office worker might realize within weeks the constraints of a desk job and yearn for more activity. Employment is an important part of our lives. It is, for most of our adult lives, our most continuous productive activity. We want to make good choices based on the right criteria.

If you have a low tolerance for risk, a job based on commission will certainly be very anxiety-provoking. If being near your family is important, issues of relocation could present a decision crisis for you. If you're an adventurous person, a job with frequent travel would provide needed excitement and be very desirable. The importance of income, the need to continue your education, your personal health situation—all of these have an impact on whether the job you are considering will ultimately meet your needs. Unless you've spent some time understanding and thinking about these issues, it will be difficult to evaluate offers you do receive.

More important, if you make a decision that you cannot tolerate and feel you must leave that job, you will then have both unemployment and self-esteem issues to contend with. These will combine to make the next job search tough going, indeed. So make your acceptance a carefully considered decision.

Negotiate Your Offer

It may be that there is some aspect of your job offer that is not particularly attractive to you. Perhaps there is no relocation allotment to help you move your possessions, and this presents some financial hardship for you. It may be that the health insurance is less than you had hoped. Your initial assignment may be different from what you expected, either in its location or in the duties and responsibilities that comprise it. Or it may simply be that the salary is less than you anticipated. Other considerations may be your official starting date of employment, vacation time, evening hours, dates of training programs or schools, and other concerns.

If you are considering not accepting the job because of some item or items in the job offer "package" that do not meet your needs, you should know that most employers emphatically wish that you would bring that issue to their attention. It may be that the employer can alter it to make the offer more agreeable for you. In some cases it cannot be changed. In any event the employer would generally like to have the opportunity to try to remedy a difficulty rather than risk losing a good potential employee over an issue that might have been resolved. After all, they have spent time and funds in securing your services, and they certainly deserve an opportunity to resolve any possible differences.

Honesty is the best approach in discussing any objections or uneasiness you might have over the employer's offer. Having received your formal offer in writing, contact your employer representative and indicate your particular dissatisfaction in a straightforward manner. For example, you might explain that while you are very interested in being employed by this organization, the salary (or any other benefit) is less than you have determined you require. State the terms you need, and listen to the response. You may be asked to put this in writing, or you may be asked to hold off until the firm can decide on a response. If you are dealing with a senior representative of the organization, one who has been involved in hiring for some time, you may get an immediate response or a solid indication of possible outcomes.

Perhaps the issue is one of relocation. Your initial assignment is in the Midwest, and because you had indicated a strong West Coast preference, you are surprised at the actual assignment. You might simply indicate that while you understand the need for the company to assign you based on its needs, you are disappointed and had hoped to be placed on the West Coast. You could inquire if that were still possible and, if not, would it be reasonable to expect a West Coast relocation in the future.

If your request is presented in a reasonable way, most employers will not see this as jeopardizing your offer. If they can agree to your proposal, they will. If not, they will simply tell you so, and you may choose to continue your candidacy with them or remove yourself from consideration. The choice will be up to you.

Some firms will adjust benefits within their parameters to meet the candidate's need if at all possible. If a candidate requires a relocation cost allowance, he or she may be asked to forgo tuition benefits for the first year to accomplish this adjustment. An increase in life insurance may be adjusted by some other benefit trade-off; perhaps a family dental plan is not needed. In these decisions you are called upon, sometimes under time pressure, to know how you value these issues and how important each is to you.

Many employers find they are more comfortable negotiating for candidates who have unique qualifications or who bring especially needed expertise to the organization. Employers hiring large numbers of entry-level college graduates may be far more reluctant to accommodate any changes in offer conditions. They are well supplied with candidates with similar education and experience so that if rejected by one candidate, they can draw new candidates from an ample labor pool.

Compare Offers

The condition of the economy, the job seeker's academic major and particular geographic job market, and individual needs and demands for certain employment conditions may not provide more than one job offer at a time. Some job seekers may feel that no reasonable offer should go unaccepted for the simple fear there won't be another.

In a tough job market, or if the job you seek is not widely available, or when your job search goes on too long and becomes difficult to sustain financially and emotionally, it may be necessary to accept an inferior offer. The alternative is continued unemployment. Even here, when you feel you don't have a choice, you can at least understand that in accepting this particular offer, there may be limitations and conditions you don't appreciate. At the time of acceptance, there were no other alternatives, but you can begin to use that position to gain the experience and talent to move toward a more attractive position.

Sometimes, however, more than one offer is received, and the candidate has the luxury of choice. If the job seeker knows what he or she wants and has done the necessary self-assessment honestly and thoroughly, it may be clear that one of the offers conforms more closely to those expressed wants and needs.

However, if, as so often happens, the offers are similar in terms of conditions and salary, the question then becomes which organization might provide the necessary climate, opportunities, and advantages for your professional development and growth. This is the time when solid employer research and astute questioning during the interviews really pay off. How much did you learn about the employer through your own research and skillful questioning? When the interviewer asked during the interview "Do you have any questions?" did you ask the kinds of questions that would help resolve a choice between one organization and another? Just as an employer must decide among numerous applicants, so must the applicant learn to assess the potential employer. Both are partners in the job search.

Reneging on an Offer

An especially disturbing occurrence for employers and career counseling professionals is when a job seeker formally (either orally or by written contract) accepts employment with one organization and later reneges on the agreement and goes with another employer.

There are all kinds of rationalizations offered for this unethical behavior. None of them satisfies. The sad irony is that what the job seeker is willing to do to the employer—make a promise and then break it—he or she would be outraged to have done to him- or herself: have the job offer pulled. It is a very bad way to begin a career. It suggests the individual has not taken the time to do the necessary self-assessment and self-awareness exercises to think and judge critically. The new offer taken may, in fact, be no better or worse than the one refused. You should be aware that there have been incidents of legal action following job candidates' reneging on an offer. This adds a very sour note to what should be a harmonious beginning of a lifelong adventure.

PART TWO

THE CAREER PATHS

5

Introduction to the History Career Paths

Who can deny the excitement and lure of history? After all, history is quite simply everything that has ever happened! The events, personalities, discoveries, and continuing mysteries are endlessly fascinating. And with increasingly sophisticated tools for revealing the facts of history and sharing them within the academic community as well as the public at large, the study of history is more exciting than ever.

History and Changing Technology

Advances in technology have markedly changed the way history is studied and taught. *The Chronicle of Higher Education*, among other publications, frequently carries stories that illustrate the relevance of studying history, the excitement and interest in applying new technology to examining the past, a glimpse into the future of the academic study of history, and a suggestion of the controversy all this change can entail. These articles outline the use of media, especially CD-ROMs and online databases, for making documents, data, and even the sights and sounds of history available to even larger audiences.

The age of dusty old textbooks is itself becoming history. Increasingly, textbooks housed on CD-ROMs contain simulations and role-playing exercises that allow students to experience how history actually takes place. They can participate in the choices and decision making of the historical figures they study, which results in greater engagement with, interest in, and understanding of the forces that shaped the present. Student response is positive and the visual and auditory enhancement of learning is entirely consistent with the preferred medium of information and entertainment transfer.

One problem noted in the *Chronicle* articles is a generational gap that currently exists between faculty who are not passionate about the use of computers and others who embrace advanced technologies. Other issues include the cost of subscribing to these items and the growing amount of storage space these databases demand. Currently, the storage and computer use are being supplied by university computer administrators, but that may change. Some scholars question the reliability and authenticity of electronically retrieved documents. Many issues remain to be solved, but the future for history is certain to include electronic and printed resources.

Technology also makes new demands on budgets that support the work of archivists, curators, and information specialists of all kinds, as new technology is never inexpensive. Information storage and retrieval will continue to be altered as we learn the best ways to store, preserve, and make this material available to the public. Accuracy and reliability of information sourcing will come under new scrutiny and will add to the critical review of these materials by information specialists.

History and Controversy

Anyone who studies history realizes it is not without controversy. That controversy will continue into the future, as has been suggested in the discussion on advanced technology. Political controversy may exist as well. As U.S. presidents make a considered choice for the position of archivist of the United States, they must ensure that whoever is chosen has the following qualifications: demonstrated professional expertise in history, archival theory and practice, or a related field; national stature among archivists, historians, and other professionals concerned with the integrity of federal records; successful experience in administering programs with responsibility for cultural or informational resources; and demonstrated understanding of archival concerns and of the role of historical research in documenting federal policies, programs, and actions.

Why the concern? The federal archivist is responsible for the housing, preservation, and availability of federal records to scholars, legislators, and the general public. He or she also oversees the presidential libraries, regional archives, and other records centers. With the Freedom of Information Act (FOIA) and the interest of journalists in past administrations, military actions, and, most recently, governmental involvement in the use of radiation experiments on human subjects, it is critical that the archivist be above politics and of unimpeachable integrity.

Consider the Future for History Majors

It has been said that history is concerned with "the memory of things said and done." Like so many liberal arts majors, the study of history is often targeted by those questioning its career relevance. The following chapters will fully illustrate the wonderful opportunities available to you with this valuable degree. They give you detailed information on which you can begin to travel your own career path and write your own personal career history. The five options described in this book include:

1. Nonclassroom education
2. Curatorial and archival management
3. Information specialization
4. Business administration and management
5. Teaching

Consider the implications of just the new technology for the career paths we outline. For educators of all kinds, classroom teachers as well as interpreters and guides, these new technologies allow history to truly come alive in sight and sound for learners. The use and ability to draw from these online systems and CD-ROM technologies will have a corresponding demand for in-service training for all types of instructors as they learn to master this technology and bring it to their students and their classroom, be it a traditional learning site or a field experience.

Now, begin exploring for yourself the innumerable byways offered by each of the paths described here.

6

Path I: Nonclassroom Education

Try to picture yourself in one or more of the following scenes:

- **Scene 1.** A group of ministers is visiting the museum where you work as an educational assistant. They are filled with enthusiasm and ask challenging questions about the traveling exhibit of the Dead Sea scrolls, which is temporarily on display. All your research and communication skills come into play in a lively and sophisticated exchange of information.
- **Scene 2.** A room full of noisy, excited children is visiting you for the morning at a building in Colonial Williamsburg where you, in costume, walk them through room after room of carefully reconstructed eighteenth-century living arrangements. You tell them stories of the people who may have lived there and what they did, and you explain the difference in Colonial life and modern living.
- **Scene 3.** Look out! Leading people on tours of indoor and outdoor environmental exhibits that include nature trails and aquatic exhibits takes careful footing and a whole new range of other skills on top of that. If you like the outdoors and enjoy sharing what you know with visitors, building exhibits, and writing grants, maybe you can see yourself here.

For history majors who want to educate, teach, and guide others, but not in the classroom, this career path offers all the rich rewards of teaching, often in a less-structured environment and with a volunteer audience that's enthusiastic and interested. What's more, you'll continue learning yourself. In this career path you will discover that traditional education continues to redefine itself. Education now extends far beyond classroom walls and, most important, draws on the resources of specialists in every area of human endeavor as collaborators and consultants in the educational process. You can join that select group of specialists that consults with the classroom teacher.

We now understand how important it is for young learners in the elementary and middle school years to listen to and hear from role models with expertise in many fields. Different voices and points of view help students develop their own critical thinking skills. Seeing different personalities, ages, and cultures present important information may be just the role modeling an individual student needs to consider his or her own career path. Classroom visits by outside experts are now commonplace. Each day, school hallways across the United States are visited by story tellers, naturalists, artists, poets, judges, tradespeople, craftspeople, farmers, and other occupational and educational representatives. These talented people want to share what they know and appreciate with a new and eager audience.

Enthusiasm is certainly important, but understanding how to structure and deliver information appropriate to varying grade levels and developmental stages is equally so. Third graders will enjoy dressing up and acting out playlets from the pilgrims' first Thanksgiving while seventh graders will find early-American farming techniques (including the use of fish as fertilizer) more fascinating. The older grades are also more interested in and better able to handle the realities of pilgrim–Native American relations or the cold, hard truth that the first Thanksgiving did not include turkey.

Knowing what you want to accomplish, what you hope your groups will learn, means setting goals, learning outcomes, and planning appropriate exercises. To assess your accomplishments and your growing expertise, you'll want some kind of evaluation instrument, however simple. This could range from the hysterical cheering following "Did you have a good time?" to a simple form for older students or adults to fill out. Teaching aids, use of media, and additional reading lists will all help the classroom teacher expand and build on your lessons.

For the classroom teacher, your expertise as a visitor brings a whole new dimension of learning to the students. It's exciting for the schoolteacher to see the changes in response and adaptability of students to a different instructor. Each student comes to you with a clean slate; consequently you treat him or her differently from the teachers who know the academic and behavioral history. In addition to your specialized content knowledge, your presence, voice, orientation to the material, and interaction with the class help these young pupils prepare for other learning experiences and other teachers.

In the high school years, as students begin to become increasingly concerned with the future, possible college choices, or vocational options, the opportunity to see and meet role models from a variety of occupations is a window on the world. In addition to the reason for your visit, you also present a role model as a working man or woman in an area of employment many students might not have heard of. Perhaps you are a representative from a natural history museum who has been invited to do a program for high school juniors. Your topic is "Whale Bone Carvings of Eighteenth-Century New England." Perhaps you'll bring along some atmosphere: a recording of waves crashing and water lapping against the side of the hull of the wooden whaling vessel. Perhaps some faintly heard sea shanties. You darken the classroom and light some candles or effect the dim light of lanterns to demonstrate the conditions under which some of these magnificent carvings were created. Of course, you'll bring samples to pass about and maybe give students the opportunity to try their hand at carving something themselves out of a comparable material.

Literature, museum studies, economics, social and cultural anthropology, art, craft, and history all prove rich fodder for young minds, and a visit such as the one described can leave an indelible impression. It is also important for your temporary students to meet and see educators from outside the classroom whose expertise is solid but whose pupils are constantly changing. They see someone creating a career from something he or she loves. They begin to understand learning can happen everywhere and throughout life. Your visit may suggest possibilities for exploration they had not imagined. They will gain from you the insight that learning does not have to take place in a classroom. Your students may be inspired to develop interests and avocational or educational pursuits that will be with them their entire lives as a source of true enrichment and pleasure.

The broadening mission of education is one of the principal motivations behind this collaboration with educators from outside the classroom. Teachers realize that they cannot do it all by themselves, and that scores of talented individuals will work with them to excite these young minds. You will be seen as a professional colleague and an important part of the educational network.

There is yet another valuable reason behind our growing dependence upon educators whose arena is not in the schools. We increasingly realize the fragility and vulnerability of our planet and its people. Never have our resources and heritage been more important to us and more subject to the stresses and strains of humanity. The preservation of the condor, the maintenance and restoration of great architecture, all the perishable remains of culture are vulnerable. We now understand the importance of protecting our historic sites, of preserving our natural wetlands, of providing resources for our natural flora and fauna, and of recognizing and celebrating the rich legacy of all our ancestors and their contributions and impact on our present lives.

The role the nonclassroom educator plays is vital, and, like the ripples across the pond that follow any disturbance of the water's surface, you often cannot and will not know the full effects of your interaction with your learners. Depending upon your setting and your presentation you may inspire hobbies, personal study regimens, or entire changes in a way of living. Whatever your effect, you will assuredly enhance and enlarge what has been learned through the traditional classroom and bring to life with a special vividness a new learning experience.

Definition of the Career Path

One of the most exciting aspects of using your history background in nonclassroom education is the incredible and unlimited variety of settings, instructional modes, and subject areas. With no difficulty whatsoever, the following brief list of possibilities was assembled from a variety of easily accessible job listings.

With such a varied list of job announcements (including some that we are certain you wish you could apply for), you might well ask, is there any commonality? What are the linking elements in the career of the nonclassroom educator? What kinds of general statements can be made about so many different positions? Consider the following:

Education Coordinator. Living history farm with agricultural tools collection and historic house. Plan family programs, liaison with teachers, manage classroom outreach program, develop interpretive materials, write grants. Flex schedule including some weekend work. Req B.A. in history, agriculture, museum studies, or museum education. Résumé, letter, and references to director of education (state historical society) . . .

Community Educator. Under direction of curator of education, assist in the implementation of programs to promote greater use of museum's resources in college teaching. Three-year, grant-funded position. B.A. required, M.A. in art history preferred, museum education experience preferred; maturity, interpersonal skills, and attention to detail essential. Send letter and résumé to (college) . . .

Program Director. Private museum noted as the birthplace of America's foremost portrait painter and for its operational 18th-century water-powered snuff mill. Located in rural community. Active interpretation program goes on from early spring to late fall. Small boats available for recreational use. Year-round position with housing provided. Salary negotiable. Good communication skills a must. Record keeping, garden maintenance, groundskeeping, general maintenance are all phases of the job. Submit résumé to trustees, . . .

Gallery Assistant. At the Old State House, assist in daily operations of the museum in areas of interpretation, visitors' services, monitoring of galleries. Gallery assistant is in daily contact with the public in the galleries or visitor orientation area. Also works directly with Department of Public Programs and volunteers. Weekend and some holiday hours required. Letter and résumé to . . .

- **Focused fields of study.** Unlike your classroom counterparts, you can focus quite specifically on a period in history, a particular person, a piece of architectural history, an environmental domain (wetland, forest, and so forth) and develop your acumen in that regard.
- **Age-specific populations.** In most of the ads listed, there are definite age parameters, which may appeal to you if you have had experience working with particular age groups.
- **Sense of excitement and adventure.** In most situations, a visit to where you work is a highlight or treat for your clientele, be it schoolchildren or a family outing. Your audiences will be enthusiastic and you will find that atmosphere infects you as well.
- **Levels of activity.** Many of these postings indicate or suggest heightened levels of activity and some make explicit statements about walking, stairs, and other physical demands. Some of this is discussed in the section that follows. Here, the important point to remember is that your classroom is more interactive and may involve more movement and energy than a traditional setting.

Working Conditions

How does having your own apartment on the grounds of a historic home and gardens sound? Or, can you imagine spending your day helping animated young schoolchildren appreciate the life of a Colonial family? Maybe your interest is in designing curricula, planning events, or organizing programs for young people of all ages. Some history majors would love to work outside, educating others about our natural history, the environment, or Native American customs.

The working conditions in this career path are defined by each individual position, and very often you will find some mention of schedule, hours, accommodation, and targeted populations in the job posting itself. Your self-assessment is important here as you will need to match your own wants, needs, skills, and abilities against the varying demands of each position. There are many working conditions to consider as you explore the world of nonclassroom education. Consider each of the following sections to see how well the job seems to "fit."

- **Public presentations.** How much public presentation does the job require, and how do you feel about that? How successful has that kind of activity been for you in the past? Will presentations be throughout the day or will they be punctuation marks in a day filled with other activities? Will you enjoy "being on" as much as the job requires, or will you find that role fatiguing?
- **Curriculum development/program planning.** If curriculum development and program planning are job requirements, how will that suit you? That means research, writing, and probably significant collaboration to develop effective programs.
- **Teamwork.** What team experiences have you had with important activities to judge your ability in this new role? Have you tended to be a "loner" or an autonomous worker in past jobs, or do you enjoy being part of a larger work unit? Will this behind the scenes work be satisfying to you, or will you be anxious to be with the public?
- **Irregular hours.** Because many facilities that seek to educate the public are open both during the school week for educational trips and on weekends for family excursions, nonclassroom educational positions frequently require some weekend hours.
- **Continuing education.** Another important factor to seriously consider is the continuing education demands of these positions. As with any educator role, the teachers themselves must continue to learn. You'll be pursuing your own self-education, year-round, on the time period, peoples, or artifacts your job deals with, in addition to conferences, seminars, and formal training programs to increase your expertise in the field. A teacher, by virtue of his or her profession, must remain a student.
- **Versatility and unpredictability.** The watchword of jobs such as these is "expect the unexpected." Your classroom is open to anyone and the public is a mysterious variable. Each group you lead will be different, and though you will come to expect and be wonderfully adept at answering those famous questions, each day will bring new challenges in the public's behavior, understanding of what you are trying to communicate, and appreciation for your field. Nonclassroom educators must enjoy the unpredictability of the public equally as much as they enjoy their subject matter.

Training and Qualifications

You probably have many questions about your readiness for any of these positions. As you read the job ads, chances are quite high that you've seen more than one job that sounds "perfect." You are probably wishing the authors had listed exactly where that job was located! By the time you read this chapter, those particular jobs have been filled. Never fear, for each day, each week, and each month bring more positions onto the market in this growing and exciting field.

Your questions remain, however. Your history study in college has been typically broad and though you have favorite topics and periods, they don't coincide with any of these jobs. Is that a problem? Absolutely not. In almost every situation you've seen advertised, be it historic home, children's museum, private collection, National Park position, or environmental center, your study skills will be put to new use as you master the research, historical background, personalities, and artifacts associated with your new employment.

In the case of tours, you will probably find "scripts" prepared that you may tailor to suit your individual style of presentation, and you may enjoy a period of training from your predecessor or another employee who has done this job. In most cases, your interpretation is limited only by your own willingness to research your subject and incorporate that material into your teaching and a corresponding need to be accurate with your facts and pay attention to details.

Earnings

Earnings packages for nonclassroom educators vary dramatically and may include important conditions of employment that need to be weighed against your salary. There may be room and/or board, long days out-of-doors, or continual stair climbing as you lead visitors on tours. Carefully weigh your needs, the job demands, and the experience you'll gain before making a decision.

The range is amazingly wide, from minimum wage tour guides to National Park positions with starting salaries of approximately $46,000 to $60,000 plus benefits in 2006. The size of the employer has much to do with entry-level salary ranges. In 2006, the Smithsonian had history education specialist positions for bachelor's degree candidates that cited a range of approximately $66,000 to $86,000 with most entry-level candidates falling at the midpoint within that range. A smaller institution, perhaps a state historical society with a comprehensive education program, would have starting salaries for educators in the mid to high twenties. Some historical sites with local or regional appeal hire costumed interpreters at hourly wages, approximating an annual salary in the high teens.

It's difficult to make sweeping generalizations about a field where required training, job demands, activity level, and possible prerequisites vary so dramatically from site to site. It is encouraging that the field of nonclassroom education is increasingly recognized for its value and importance in conveying information that profoundly affects the recipient's learning through channels outside the traditional classroom setting.

Career Outlook

The career outlook for the talented nonclassroom educator is promising, although actual job prospects vary from one region to another and with changing economic conditions. Be it a restored Shaker village, historic mill reconstruction, art gallery, museum education program of any type, wetlands reclamation project, or costumed interpretation, the variety, number, and scope of these professions will lead to challenging career possibilities grow as North Americans continue to be interested in what is educational, entertaining, and enjoyable as a pastime.

Gone are the days when the public would suffer a self-guided tour with printed literature. Though many still prefer this, many others opt for a guide, a docent, an interpreter, or an information coordinator to make their experience worthwhile. For young people, this often means interactive programs. For adults, it frequently means specific answers to countless questions that have real meaning for the person asking them. No matter what the age or experience, the addition of your role as a nonclassroom educator heightens and enhances the experience for everyone!

Strategies for Finding the Jobs

If you can't picture yourself sitting behind a desk for most of your workday, you can use your degree in history to work in a nonclassroom educational setting. Outlined here is a four-pronged strategy you can implement to position yourself more competitively in the marketplace. Consider undertaking these tasks:

Learn About Educational Theory and Process

Unless you have been granted or are eligible for teacher certification, you will want to learn more about educational theory and the educational process. Because many of the positions outlined in this path either oversee or provide educational programming, it is important to know how to reach the audiences you are trying to educate.

Gain an understanding of the differences in learning styles for different ages and how to appeal to the various ways in which we all learn. You can use a number of methods to acquire this information.

1. **Become a critical observer of other nonclassroom educators.** When you attend meetings, workshops, and seminars or even watch educational television, note how information is conveyed, how media is employed to illustrate certain points, and what techniques are used to assess learning outcomes.

2. **Read.** The library has some excellent resource books on how to construct education programs that include setting reasonable learning goals, developing learning activities to further those goals, and testing or evaluating for learning outcomes that you expect from your presentation. Create your own bibliography of good instructional books and put it in your portfolio. Be ready to discuss your own position on effective designs for learning.

3. **Enroll in a continuing education course or professional seminar on conducting effective workshops.** These are often full-day programs that cover all aspects of effective program design and delivery, and you will be able to document this formal training on your résumé. It might also stimulate you to do some further study on your own.

4. **Think also about acquiring some good media technology skills.** Too often, the presenter's inability with a computerized projection device can mar an otherwise strong program. Your college or university or local high school may have a media specialist on the staff who would be willing to volunteer some time to acquaint you with the most common equipment and how to operate it effectively.

Acquire a Specialized Knowledge That Complements Your Study of History

As you have seen in the job descriptions, some require knowledge in areas not covered in a traditional history curriculum. Some positions require knowledge of art history, natural history, or the environment, while others ask for computer or media skills. The academic minor you choose could play a critical role in helping you acquire the specialized knowledge you'll need to gain employment in certain types of positions.

If you have already graduated, consider taking continuing-education courses at a nearby college or university to enhance your skills. Or consider adding to your portfolio of skills by attending a one-time seminar or workshop. Many professional associations notify members of and offer training and educational opportunities in this more-intensive, shorter format. Check the association information at the end of this chapter for those organizations that offer seminars, workshops, or other training opportunities.

Do an Internship or Volunteer Your Time

There are a range of settings in which nonclassroom educational programs are offered, and each requires a specialized knowledge. Your academic work is important, but gaining actual work experience in the field is also critical to your job search success. By gaining work experience in a specific type of setting you will be able to test your decision by seeing if you like the work, you will gain hands-on experience to add to your résumé, and you will make important contacts who may be willing to help you in your search for professional employment.

Many excellent books and websites can help you locate actual internships. These resources also help you understand the types of employers that work with interns. Visit your college careers library for copies of *The Vault Guide to Internships* or *The Internship Bible*. You can find many other resources both online and on the shelves, so be sure to ask the career professional or librarian you are working with for other resources.

Use Both Reactive and Proactive Job Search Techniques

Your job search should begin with a review of published job listings. You'll get a good sense of the types of jobs that are available and the range of titles used to describe these jobs. In addition, you'll become intimately familiar with duties associated with each type of job and the salary range for the geographic area you're examining. Some sources for actual job listings can be found in the section listing professional associations. Other excellent job listings include:

CareerBuilder.com (careerbuilder.com)
Current Jobs in Art (graduatejobs.com/art)
Current Jobs for Graduates (graduatejobs.com)
JobHunt (job-hunt.org)
Environmental Career Opportunities (ecojobs.com)

Aviso: A Monthly Dispatch from the American Association of Museums
   (aam-us/jobHQ)
All Canadian Jobs (allcanadianjobs.com)
Best Jobs Canada (bestjobsca.com)
Canadajobs.com (canadajobs.com)
Eluta Canada (eluta.ca)

Using information contained in this path and in the job descriptions you read, you'll be able to create a focused résumé that describes how you can help accomplish the goals of the organizations you are approaching and learn to speak directly to employer needs in an interview situation.

But don't limit your search to simply responding to job advertisements. Be sure to use your college alumni network to begin developing contacts who are currently employed at the type of organization you would like to work for. Use other techniques described in the networking chapter of this book to enhance your proactive job search activities.

Possible Employers

Museums are, of course, one of the major employers for nonclassroom educators. But have you considered the other types of employers that hire people to educate the public about their histories, mission, or collections? Read on and find out more about some of them, including zoological parks, aquariums, wildlife refuges, and bird sanctuaries; arboretums, botanical and aquatic gardens, conservatories, and horticultural societies; outdoor education centers; camps; and national and state parks.

Museums

Have you ever investigated all of the different types of museums that exist in the United States and Canada? There is an institution for nearly every interest. Most often art comes to mind when we hear the word museum, but educational programs, walking tours, films, lectures, or slide shows are also offered at textile museums, children's museums, military museums, arboretums, wildlife refuges, circus museums, and sports museums.

The American Association of Museums categorizes institutions into one of fourteen groups. They include:

Art museums
Children's museums
College and university museums

Company museums
Exhibit areas
General museums
History museums
Libraries having collections of books
Libraries having collections other than books
National and state agencies, councils, and commissions
Nature centers
Park museums and visitor centers
Science museums
Specialized museums

History and specialized museums may be of particular interest to the history major; these types of facilities are divided into several subcategories in *The Official Museum Directory* (officialmuseumdir.com).

Under the history category of museums you will find, of course, history museums, but you will also see military museums and preservation projects, as well as history agencies, councils, commissions, and research institutes. Be sure to review *The Official Museum Directory* for a complete listing of their members in this category.

Agricultural museums to horological museums displaying timepieces, industrial museums to woodcarving museums, all are found in the specialized museum classification. If you have a hobby or special interest, you may be able to combine your specialized knowledge with your work in a non-classroom educational environment.

Help in Locating These Employers. If you would like to explore one of these categories of museums, the best source is the latest edition of *The Official Museum Directory*. Institutions are indexed by state and by category of institution. In addition, other listings of interest are provided, including:

Federal agencies providing museum support
Regional arts organizations
State and provincial arts or humanities agencies

Other useful resources that can be used to help you locate potential employers include your local and regional yellow pages (look under Museums) and state or regional directories of nonprofit organizations. Call your local chamber of commerce to determine whether they know of such a directory for your area. Or talk with a representative of a state, provincial, or regional museum association. The regions are:

New England Museum Association, Boston, Massachusetts
Mid-Atlantic Association of Museums, Newark, Delaware
Southeastern Museums Conference, Baton Rouge, Louisiana
Midwest Museum Conference, St. Louis, Missouri
Mountain-Plains Museum Association, Manitou Springs, Colorado
Western Museums Association, Los Angeles, California
Alberta Museums Association, Edmonton, Alberta
British Columbia Museums Association, Victoria, British Columbia
Association of Manitoba Museums, Winnipeg, Manitoba
Museum Association of Newfoundland and Labrador, St. Johns, Newfoundland
Ontario Museums Association, Toronto, Ontario
Société des musées québécois, Montreal, Quebec
Museums Association of Saskatchewan, Regina, Saskatchewan
Yukon Historical & Museums Association, Whitehorse, Yukon

Zoological Parks, Aquariums, Wildlife Refuges, and Bird Sanctuaries

If your interests lie in helping the general public understand the impact of historical events and human experiences on the living creatures with whom we share the world, you may be interested in getting involved in educational programming efforts offered at zoos, aquariums, wildlife refuges, and bird sanctuaries. Some work as guides at sites all around the United States and Canada, leading groups of interested nature and animal lovers on zoo or aquarium tours, nature walks, and wildlife education tours.

Help in Locating These Employers. An excellent resource for locating zoos and aquariums is the website of the Association of Zoos and Aquariums (aza.org). They have a zoo and aquarium locator on their site that gives a detailed précis of the facility you are researching including size, staff, equipment, exhibit information, and species exhibited. Each site also includes a hot link to the home page of the facility itself. The Canadian Association of Zoos and Aquariums (caza.ca) is a similar source of helpful information.

The Official Museum Directory also lists these types of organizations and can provide a contact name, mailing address, website listing, telephone number, and background information.

For the most part, wildlife refuge and bird sanctuary educators are public sector employees. The federal government, as well as state and local governments, hire workers to educate the public through various education programs. National agencies that hire this type of educator include the National Park Service, Parks Canada, the U.S. Fish and Wildlife Service, and the Bureau of Land Management. State or provincial departments or agencies that may provide employment opportunities include environmental protection, fish and wildlife, forestry, natural resources, and parks and recreation. Local governments that include a parks and recreation department may also hire workers for nonclassroom teaching positions. The National Audubon Society has published a comprehensive set of guides to America's wildlife refuges: *Audubon Guide to National Wildlife Refuges* (nationalwildlifeguide. com). A description of each refuge is provided, as well as directions for locating the site, hours of operation, what can be seen and done there, and contact information if you would like to learn more.

Many nonprofit organizations that were established to protect animal life or wilderness areas also run educational programs. Examples include the National Audubon Society (audubon.org), the Canadian Parks and Wilderness Society (paws.org), the Canadian Wildlife Federation (cwf-fcf.org), the National Wildlife Federation (nwf.org) and the Wildlife Conversation Society (wcs.org). You'll also want to check out the website of the U.S. Environmental Protection Agency (epa.gov) or Environment Canada (ec.gc.ca). They provide information on topics such as animal rights groups, educational organizations, and groups devoted to endangered species and wildlife preservation.

Arboretums, Botanical and Aquatic Gardens, Conservatories, and Horticultural Societies

Have you ever enjoyed walking through a forest of enormous redwood trees or the high trails of the Blue Ridge Mountains? Or enjoyed smelling the rich pines of coastal woodlands? You can combine your love for or interest in living botanical environments with your history degree to educate people who share these same interests.

Help in Locating These Employers. The American Horticulture Society (ahs.org) and various provincial societies in Canada can be good sources of information about potential employers. If you are interested in working at a botanical garden, you can join the American Association of Botanical Gardens and Arboreta (aabga.org). *The Official Museum Directory* also contains contact information for these types of facilities.

Outdoor Education Centers

Have you ever participated in a leadership training program that included a ropes course or visited a center that offered a year-round program in environmental education? Both of these types of settings are included in what we are calling outdoor education. Each type of facility employs workers who are dedicated to the mission of the organization, and many of these people have bachelor's degrees. A recent review of the credentials of an adventure center's employees revealed that nine of the sixteen had either a B.A. or a B.S., and all had a deep commitment to outdoor education.

Help in Locating These Employers. Employment opportunities exist in many places and are called by different names, so be sure to follow up on lots of different leads. Year-round environmental-education centers employ people like yourself, and you can locate them by contacting the North American Association for Environmental Education located in Troy, Ohio. You can also contact the Educational Resources Information Center (ERIC) resources at your college or public library.

Additionally, state and province departments of natural resources or environmental protection often offer ongoing educational programs. Check with these agencies or with state or provincial employment sites to find out about job vacancies. Environmental issues are a major concern in our society, and much is being written about careers in this area, so be sure to ask for assistance in locating the many additional resources available to you.

Camps

Camping is a long-standing North American tradition; there are summer resident and day camps, church camps, and travel and trip camps sponsored under public and private auspices. If you are interested in becoming a part of the educational efforts provided through the camping experience, many opportunities are available, especially during the summer months. Year-round opportunities are not as abundant but are available.

Help in Locating These Employers. One resource to begin with is the database published by the American Camp Association (acacamps.org). This site provides contact information that you can use to find out about jobs that are, primarily, available during the summer months. A Web search under one of the metasearch engines such as Google or Yahoo using the words *marine and environmental camps* will deliver a number of options in camp programs for all ages across North America, providing opportunities for nonclassroom educational efforts.

National, State, and Provincial Parks

Nearly every national and state or provincial park has a visitor center that is the focal point for educational programs. These park systems employ people to educate individuals and groups who visit the park about special features found there such as spouting geysers at Yellowstone National Park, mammoth redwoods at Yosemite National Park, glaciers of Georges Island in Nova Scotia, rare prairie grasses of Grasslands National Park in Saskatchewan, and lofty sand dunes at Cape Hatteras National Seashore. Many individuals begin their government career in national or state parks as summer park rangers. Those who "pay their dues" have the advantage of previous government employment as they are being considered for available full-time openings.

Help in Locating These Employers. Each year the U.S. Department of the Interior, National Park Service, advertises seasonal park ranger positions by notifying career offices across the country. Information on locations offering employment and application forms are available through these offices as well as federal job information centers. Competition for these entry-level jobs is keen, so begin your search early, carefully complete the application, and follow up with the parks you are most interested in. Full-time positions are advertised in publications and websites such as *Federal Jobs Digest*, USA Jobs (usajobs.opm.gov), GovJobs.com (govjobs.com), All Canadian Jobs (allcanadianjobs.com), and Best Jobs Canada (bestjobsca.com).

Possible Job Titles

Job titles in nonclassroom educational programming will vary depending on the type of employer and role within the educational effort (administering versus teaching), but often-seen job titles include the following:

Administrative assistant
Coordinator of interpretation and visitor services
Coordinator of school and youth programs
Director of education (museum)
Director of educational programs
Director of visitor services
Education coordinator
Education specialist
Educational programs coordinator
Educator
Environmental education instructor/teacher
Executive director

Field instructor
Interpreter/caretaker
Interpretive guide
Museum assistant
Museum educator
Nature education instructor
Nature interpreter
Outdoor education instructor
Outreach assistant
Park ranger
Programs coordinator
Project planner and coordinator
School programs assistant
Urban park ranger

Related Occupations

The nonclassroom educator uses a variety of skills and many are directly transferable to a variety of other jobs. These positions require designing, organizing, and implementing programs; making public presentations; and acting as a public relations representative. Review the list that follows, and for the titles that are unfamiliar to you, do some investigating to see if they are job possibilities you should consider.

Career counselor
Caseworker
Classroom teacher
Conference coordinator
Educational equipment and supplies salesperson
Financial aid counselor
Human resources professional
Librarian
Public relations specialist
Training specialist
Travel agent

Professional Associations

Many different professional associations have been listed here, and some provide services or publications that you might like to use. Contact those you want to find out more about and ask them to send you information. If you are currently a student, you may be able to initially join the organization for a modest student membership fee. Make sure you know what benefits you'll get from joining a particular association, and ask specifically how the organization can help you in your job search. Many provide job listings in their newsletter, or they may have a job-placement service available to members. Read on and think about whether membership would benefit you in your job search.

American Association for Museum Volunteers
c/o American Association of Museums
1575 I St. NW
Washington, DC 20005
ansp.org/hosted/agmv
Members/Purpose: Affiliate committee of the American Association of Museums. Serves as forum and source information for museum volunteers.
Training: None
Journal/Publication: *AAMV Newsletter*; books on museum volunteerism; *Museum Volunteer Handbook*
Job Listings: None

American Association for State and Local History
1717 Church St.
Nashville, TN 37203
aaslh.org
Members/Purpose: Organizations of educators, historians, writers, and other individuals; state and local historical societies; agencies and institutions interested in improving the study of state and local history in the United States and Canada, and assisting historical organizations in improving their public services.
Training: Conducts seminars and workshops.
Journal/Publications: *History News*; *Dispatch*; reports; technical leaflets; and other publications
Job Listings: None

American Association of Museums
1575 I St. NW, Suite 400
Washington, DC 20005
aam-us.org

Members/Purpose: Art, history, and science museums; art associations and centers; historic houses and societies; preservation projects; planetariums; zoos; aquariums; botanical gardens; college and university museums; and others interested in the museum field.
Training: None
Journals/Publications: *Aviso*; *Museum News*; *jobHQ*
Job Listings: Maintains placement services for museum professionals; see *Aviso* for employment opportunities in museums.

American Camp Association
5000 State Rd. 67 North
Martinsville, IN 46151-7902
acacamps.org
Members/Purpose: Camp owners, directors, counselors, camps, businesses, and students interested in resident and day-camp programs for youth and adults. Conducts camp standards and camp director certification programs. Offers information services in several areas including educational programs.
Training: None
Journals/Publications: *Camping Magazine*; *The Campline*; annual buyer's guide
Job Listings: Sponsors placement service.

American Public Gardens Association (formerly American Association of Botanical Gardens and Arboreta)
100 West 10th St., Suite 614
Wilmington, DE 19801
publicgardens.org
Members/Purpose: Directors and staffs of botanical gardens, arboretums, institutions maintaining or conducting horticultural courses, and others.
Training: None
Journals/Publications: *AABGA Newsletter*; *Public Garden*; internship directory; salary survey
Job Listings: Offers online career center with job postings.

Association of Art Museum Directors
120 E. 65th St., Suite 520
New York, NY 10022
aamd.org
Members/Purpose: Chief staff officers of major art museums.
Training: None

Journals/Publications: *Professional Practices in Art Museums*; *Art Museum Salary Survey*; reports and position papers
Job Listings: None

Association for Living Historical, Farm, and Agricultural Museums
8774 Route 45 NW
North Bloomfield, OH 44450
alhfam.org
Members/Purpose: Provides a central repository of information on plants, animals, tools, and implements used in farming in the past; assists farms and museums in securing information; accredits living historical farms and museums; joins in publicizing the farms and museums.
Training: None
Journals/Publications: Convention proceedings; *ALHFAM Bulletin*; Guidebook to ALHFAM Institutional members
Job Listings: None

Association of Zoos and Aquariums
8403 Colesville Rd., Suite 710
Silver Spring, MD 20910
aza.org
Members/Purpose: Zoological parks and aquariums; supports promoting zoos and aquariums for educational and scientific interpretation of nature conservation and for public recreation and cultural pursuits.
Training: None
Journals/Publications: Conference proceedings; *Connect Magazine*; *Contact* newsletter
Job Listings: Posted online.

Canadian Parks and Recreation Association
404-2197 Riverside Dr.
Ottawa, ON K1H 7X3
cpra.ca
Members/Purpose: Serves parks and recreation professionals located in more than 2,600 communities in Canada; collaborates with thirteen provincial and territorial parks and recreation associations along with other organizations operating in the recreation, physical activity, environmental, facilities, sports, public health, crime prevention, and social services arenas; plays an advocacy role on the benefits of parks and recreation services and provides members with a variety of information and services.

Training: Sponsors conferences, workshops and other professional development opportunities including the Canadian Playground Safety Institute and Web-hosted discussion forums.
Journals/Publications: *CPRA E-News*; e-mail updates; annual report
Job Listings: Offers a job and résumé database.

The Conservation Fund
1655 N. Fort Myer Dr., Suite 1300
Arlington, VA 22209
conservationfund.org
Members/Purpose: Promotes the conservation of land and water resources; works to safeguard wildlife habitat, working landscapes, community "green space," and historic sites.
Training: None
Journals/Publications: *Common Ground*; *Corporate Highlights*
Job Listings: None

Ethnic Cultural Preservation Council
6500 S. Pulaski Rd.
Chicago, IL 60629
Members/Purpose: North American ethnic museums, other museums, historical societies, libraries, archives, fraternal organizations, universities, university libraries, and cultural centers; functions as vehicle for other ethnic and nonethnic groups to become viable art and education centers in their communities.
Training: Sponsors seminars and exhibits.
Journals/Publications: None
Job Listings: None

Intermuseum Conservation Association
2915 Detroit Ave.
Cleveland, OH 44113
ica-artconversation.org
Members/Purpose: Performs the examination and treatment of works of art, inspection and maintenance of collections, and research and education in art conservation technology.
Training: Conducts seminars for museum professionals.
Journals/Publications: None
Job Listings: Has newsletter with job listings for members.

National Association for Interpretation
P.O. Box 2246
Ft. Collins, CO 80522
interpnet.com
Members/Purpose: Specialists who prepare exhibits and conduct programs at information centers maintained by public and private institutions; persons engaged in education programs at museums, zoos, parks, arboretums, botanical gardens, historical sites, schools, and camps. Seeks to advance education and develop skills in interpreting the natural, historical, and cultural environment.
Training: Provides national training opportunities; conducts regional training workshops.
Journals/Publications: Directory of members; *Legacy*; *The Interpreter*; *Journal of Interpretation Research*
Job Listings: Provides information on job opportunities through employment hotlines and listings.

National Recreation and Park Association
22377 Belmont Ridge Rd.
Ashburn, VA 20148-4150
nrpa.org
Members/Purpose: Professional park and recreation directors who provide cultural, physical, and intellectual opportunities in recreational settings throughout the country.
Training: Conducts educational sessions and research symposia at annual congressional meetings.
Journals/Publications: *Parks and Recreation*; *Journal of Leisure Research*; *Schole*; other publications including research abstracts
Job Listings: None

National Society for Park Resources
22377 Belmont Ridge Rd.
Ashburn, VA 20148-4150
nrpa.org
Members/Purpose: A professional branch of the National Recreation and Park Association; park resource managers, planners, designers, rangers, and maintenance persons; nature interpreters and persons concerned with the preservation and use of natural, recreational, historic, and cultural resources.
Training: Conducts educational seminars and training institutes.

Journals/Publications: *Parks and Recreation*; *Journal of Leisure Research*; *Schole*; *NSPR Manual of Procedures*; other publications including research abstracts

Job Listings: Publishes job opportunities.

National Wildlife Federation
11100 Wildlife Center Dr.
Reston, VA 20190
nwf.org

Members/Purpose: Federation of state and territorial conservation organizations and associate members, including individual conservationist-contributors; encourages the intelligent management of the life-sustaining resources of the earth and promotes greater appreciation of these resources, their community relationship, and wise use.

Journals/Publications: *National Wildlife*; *Ranger Rick*; *Your Big Backyard*; *Wild Animal Baby*; fact sheets, reports, and other publications

National Wildlife Refuge Association
1901 Pennsylvania Ave. NW, Suite 407
Washington, DC 20006
refugenet.com

Members/Purpose: Conservation clubs, National Audubon Society chapters, birding groups, NWR employees and retirees, and interested individuals; seeks to protect the integrity of the National Wildlife Refuge System and to increase public understanding and appreciation of it.

Training: Conducts education and information programs.

Journal/Publication: *Wildlife Refuge*

Job Listings: None

North American Association for Environmental Education
2000 P St. NW, Suite 540
Washington DC 20036
naaee.org

Members/Purpose: Individuals associated with colleges, public schools, nature centers, government agencies, and environmental organizations; associates include students in environmental education and environmental studies.

Journals/Publications: *Environmental Education Undergraduate and Graduate Programs and Faculty in the United States*; conference proceedings, monographs, and reports

Job Listings: None

Wilderness Education Association
900 E. 7th St.
Bloomington, IN 47405
wildernesseducation.org
Members/Purpose: To promote a professional approach toward outdoor leadership and improve the safety and quality of outdoor trips and enhance the conservation of the wild outdoors; trains and certifies outdoor leaders; operates in affiliation with thirty colleges, universities, and outdoor programs; conducts National Standard Program for Outdoor Leadership Certification.
Training: Offers training to employers, administrative agencies, insurance companies, and the public; sponsors special courses for experienced professionals.
Journals/Publications: *Journal of the Wilderness Education Association*; *Backcountry Classroom*
Job Listings: Job referral service for members.

World Wildlife Fund Canada
245 Eglinton Ave. East, Suite 410
Toronto, ON M4P 3J1
wwfcanada.org
Members/Purpose: Serves more than 50,000 Canadians as a member of the WWF International network; promotes conservation, biodiversity, use of renewable natural resources, and reduction of pollution and wasteful consumption.
Training: None
Journals/Publications: Offers Web-based reports and guides and a variety of print publications
Job Listings: Offers online job listings.

7

Path 2: Curatorial and Archival Management

Acommon question asked of the history major is, "Well, what are you going to do with that degree after you graduate?" As this book amply demonstrates, there's no lack of opportunities to build a career on the history degree. It has always been a superb beginning for careers in teaching, business administration and management, information specialization, and a variety of nonclassroom educational roles. Curatorial and archival work is another very fertile area of employment for a history major. Though one of the most obvious uses of a degree in history, curatorial work is often overlooked by the history major as the province of art students and archival work as the province of library or information science graduates. After reading this chapter, you may want to answer that infamous question, "What are you going to do with a history degree?" with "I'm going to become a curator!" or "I've decided to become an archivist!"

Multiple Job Roles

Thinking of curators and archivists as simply custodians of the past would be a mischaracterization. Of course both acquire objects and works; document them as to origin, composition, provenance, age, and condition; and they store them for scholars and researchers and for rotation on display. They ensure the preservation of artifacts through temperature and humidity control and scientific conservation methods, and they display and maintain these pieces for our enjoyment, wonder, and edification.

But today's curators/archivists are much, much more. They are environmentalists, historians, teachers, explorers, trainers, and impresarios. Think about these roles and review excerpts from some of these job ads.

Environmentalists

Curators and archivists have become adept at correcting and stopping ravages of dirt, smog, fumes, acid rain, and other ills on the artifacts. They also have been frequently called out of the work site to consult with municipal officials, private collectors, and the federal government on how best to preserve and maintain our existing cultural heritage.

> **Regional Museum.** Duties include stewardship, rehabilitation, and restoration of historic buildings in compliance with the philosophy of treating historic structures as the largest artifacts in collections.

Historians

Your position might be called "preservation curator" or "assistant director for historic resources," but whether or not the word *history* appears in your job title, it is very present in your work. In addition to many positions requiring you to have a history degree, there may be stipulations as to your mastery of historical facts, literature, and art of a particular period.

> **Provincial Historical Society.** Successful candidate will possess a depth of knowledge of Western Canadian history and specifically the history of the region in the nineteenth century . . .

Teachers

People visit collections and museums to learn. The curatorial and archival staffs can be among the best teachers. They have intimate knowledge of their collections and can make what was previously confusing or misunderstood coherent and explainable. They are knowledgeable and adept at connecting events, personalities, literature, and art so that we begin to understand the times, the people, and their expressive efforts.

> **Nonprofit Professional Association.** This position offers the opportunity to engage in cutting-edge continuing education programming, to establish national leadership in the field of archival education . . .

Explorers

Curators and archivists are breaking new ground each year as they stretch the traditional definitional boundaries of their jobs. New kinds of museums (computer museums, discovery museums, indigenous peoples collections) and new locations all around the world require risk takers and adventuresome types in a field where that has not been the traditional association.

> **New Wine, Food, and Arts Museum.** Excellent opportunities exist for museum professionals to join the team that will open the (new) center. This is a start-up environment.

Trainers

Exhibits are often so rich with information and detail that, without a trained guide, we would only skim the surface and leave with only a superficial understanding of what is being presented. Consequently, curators need to be skilled trainers, bringing together groups with leadership and strong interpersonal skills to enliven, entertain, and educate.

> **Large Metropolitan Museum.** Opportunity for skilled communicator with demonstrated leadership to oversee guide and volunteer programs, including supervision, training, and administration.

Impresarios

For the purpose of this career path, we have brought these two positions (curator and archivist) together because, for the history major, there is more in common between the positions than there are differences. In fact, you will find some job postings for both curators and archivists that read almost identically. But are they the same? No, they are not, although they do share many of the same concerns. Let's begin with some of the generally accepted definitions:

• **Curators:** Those engaged in operating exhibiting institutions (museums, botanical gardens, arboretums, art galleries, zoos) who direct activities concerned with acquisition, instruction, exhibition, and safekeeping of primarily three-dimensional objects; research and publication; and public service.

• **Archivists:** Individuals concerned with the identification, preservation, and use of records of enduring historical value. Archivists work for the government, colleges and universities, historical societies, museums, libraries, businesses, and religious institutions. They work with records of all types, including letters and diaries, photographs, films, sound recordings, maps, manuscripts, and machine-readable records.

A Variety of Employment Settings

The history major who pursues curatorial and archival positions will find the variety of work settings particularly exciting. You might initially consider a major museum or collection in a downtown urban area. Of course, the United States and Canada do have a significant number of important museums located in major cities, and those institutions do have large staffs. However, restored historic homes, specialized collections, smaller museums, art galleries, complete re-creations of historic working villages and towns, children's discovery centers, and countless ethnic and indigenous peoples exhibitions can be found all across this country and, in fact, the world. All require curators and archivists, as well as other types of staff positions you may find equally intriguing.

The following list demonstrates the wide variety of collections and structures available. This list is not complete; it would be impossible to stay abreast of the constantly changing world of exhibits, collections, museums, and site re-creations. The authors once came across a published "call for interested applicants for the development of a new museum dedicated to Civil War medicine."

Antiquarian and landmark societies
Art conservation laboratories
Automobile museums
Aviation museums
Centers for curatorial studies
Centers of science and industry
Children's museums
Collections built around the home and/or work of a famous person
College and university museum collections
Computer museums
Historic houses
Historical societies
Maritime museums
Museums of art

Museums of photography/moving image
Natural history museums
Oral history centers
Private collections
Railroad museums
Re-created villages
State or provincial museums
Whaling museums

Each item in this list represents not only employment possibilities, especially when the generic type of institution cited is multiplied by states, regions, or countries, but also sharp differences in degree of focus. Some museums hold broad, expansive collections of art, sculptures, furnishings, maps, films, and other items that require curators and archivists to be equally talented and adept in a variety of areas. In these museums (a state historical collection provides a good example) you will need to know prints, furniture, fabric, and paintings.

Specialized museums or smaller, more focused collections (a museum devoted to transportation or contemporary art) will, by necessity, demand not breadth but depth in their faculty and require applicants to come to the position with considerable expertise in their material.

Explore the following list and, better yet, explore some of the wonderful job postings that are available. You can find them on the Internet and in newsletters available through your career office or through the associations mentioned at the close of this chapter. Two specific websites are worth your time. First, the American Association of Museums (aam-us.org) offers a helpful online jobs center that includes both job listings and useful career information. Second, the Society of American Archivists (archivists.org) has an online employment bulletin. As with all such specialized job listings, reading the job announcements will indicate how competitive you are in the marketplace and suggest many possible paths your career may take as you grow and develop with it.

A Growing Need for Professionals

We continue to find areas of our culture that cry out for the skilled work of curatorial and archival professionals. For example, as researchers explore the role of slaves in colonial America, more and more information has emerged about the everyday lives of slaves and slave owners. Similarly, art historians continue to learn more about the artists of early North America and Canada. In many cases, such information is documented on websites where it may be studied by other researchers. Viva the Internet!

The restored National Park Service facility at Ellis Island has brought together the efforts of numerous curators and archivists eager to help tell the story of U.S. immigration in the very buildings in which it took place. One can even still walk the Stairs of Separation where immigrants, newly screened in the great Registry Hall, were shunted to railway passage and freedom or holding facilities for medical or documentation purposes, or, tragically, deportation back to their homelands. The curators and archivists of this exhibit have provided not only exhibit rooms filled with wonderful photographs but magnificent displays of artifacts such as steamship passage tickets, passport photos, great dramatic displays of actual immigrant trunks of every variety of composition, and actual recordings of immigrants describing their heartache at leaving their homelands and their fear, trepidation, and joy in arriving in the New World. But this exhibit is not just about preserving the legacy of our great diversity as a country. It records and preserves our future as well.

Definition of the Career Path

Through their collections, curators and archivists must want to connect with the public. They have stories to share about the objects they preserve, and they truly must enjoy and welcome that sharing. The following job advertisement for a curator is indicative of the qualification demands museum administrators must ask of experienced professionals seeking curator/archivist positions.

Program Coordinator. This position has primary responsibility for the interpretive programs concerned with the exhibitions and collections of the gallery and for the integration of the gallery with the intellectual, teaching, and research prerogatives of a major research university. Responsibilities include: creating discussion on campus and in the community pertaining to the exhibitions and collections on view; making the art and the ideas and cultural context they represent accessible to a diverse constituency; organization of international symposia, lecture series, courses, film series, discussion groups, docent training, and other educational programs.

You can begin developing these skills in entry-level positions. Let's look at two job postings that reveal even more surprising and interesting facts about the curator/archivist position.

Museum Assistant. The [regional] Museum seeks energetic professional to assist with all curatorial and archival activities in a multistructure National Register facility. Primary responsibilities include collections care, research, and exhibition development and design. Excellent written and verbal communications skills, familiarity with computer cataloging systems, and ability to deal effectively with the public and donors are essential. B.A. in relevant field, experience with collections management preferred.

Health Archivist. Leading health-care system is recruiting for an enthusiastic photo archivist to manage the visual resources of the archives. The archives capture the rich history of the organization since its founding in 1914. Responsibilities of this new position include create a descriptive database, develop an improved storage and conservation program, update policies and procedures, outreach to entities in the system, undertake reference work, and design exhibits. Bachelor's degree in history; experience involving photographs and visual resources, reference work, and computer database development.

Computer Skills

Looking at actual job advertisements is a window on the reality of the jobs you seek. How many of you reading these job announcements would have realized the importance of computer skills? If you stop to think about it, the collection and retrieval of data, similar to research you did in college, are intrinsic to the study of history and one of the foremost skills you bring to any of the career paths. The computer adds a level of technology that allows you to work faster, smarter, and more efficiently than you otherwise might. If you're interested in curatorial and archival positions, you'll want to ensure that you acquire the necessary computer skills. In the section on qualifications, we discuss this and other important and necessary attributes you'll want to acquire before leaving college, which will help you compete for entry-level work.

Communication Skills

What else do these ads tell us about the jobs? Developing exhibits, helping to guide visitors through a historic home, working on the computer, and caring for and documenting collections all add up to a busy, diverse, and active career. It's a far cry from how many people think of a curator's or archivist's job.

Both of these jobs are more about the present than the past. It's about bringing the past into the present, communicating it, and making it real,

immediate, and helpful to us. It is not an exercise in simply displaying artifacts under glass for visitors to pass by in varying stages of bewilderment.
Real exhibits explain, dramatize, and make understandable what seems at first
to be remote and obscure.

Exhibit Design

The advertisements in this section announced that the job holder will help
in exhibit design. Design is an area that can help us appreciate and understand the past as well as the objects featured. Perhaps you are helping to
mount an exhibit of Egyptian artifacts discovered in the ancient pyramids.
Exhibit room walls and public foyers might be repainted to resemble the magnificent frescoes of the tombs, helping exhibit visitors to appreciate the color,
symbolism, and figurative motifs of the time. The exhibit itself might be
dimly lit overall, with effective spotlighting on the objects, as if the exhibit-
goers were discovering the artifacts themselves in the vaults of the pyramids,
adding to the excitement and drama of the collection and helping people to
focus on the intricacy, detail, and beauty of the pieces being displayed.

Begin Building Your Career

The road to a successful career in either curatorship or archival studies is a
lengthy process of building expertise and experiences. Extensive study, field
trips, the opportunity to mount or catalog a collection, each of these experiences enriches your professional life and will add elements to your résumé
that may be important for promotion or job change.

As you learn more about your job and the dimensions it offers you in terms
of a career, you may find yourself moving along a specific career path within
this field. Let's look at some of the traditional positions, highlighting their
duties and responsibilities and role in the overall function of an institution.

Entry-Level Curators

Curators are charged with the care and stewardship of a collection. To ensure
not only good accessibility to the collection they maintain, but also a high
quality exhibit, entry-level curators must understand the basics of preservation and maintenance methods, assist in developing and implementing interpretive programs, and help in researching and documenting collections.

Curators

Professional curators are true scholars who, in addition to many of the
duties listed under entry-level curatorship, both speak and write frequently

on their chosen field. As this is often a management position, they must also develop strong organizational, budgetary, and supervisory talents to schedule and train staff, maintain operating budgets, and deal with a variety of support personnel. Additional skills may involve grant writing, connoisseurship, research, and buying and selling elements to enhance the collections.

Entry-Level Archivists

The duties of the archivist involve maintaining control, both physical and intellectual, over noncurrent permanent records of individuals, groups, institutions, and governments. Entry-level archivists work under close supervision on tasks of limited scope. Requirements will include computer capabilities, physical abilities in lifting up to fifty pounds, and communication skills for working with other team members and serving the public.

Archivists

A professional archivist has extensive knowledge about the historical context in which given records were created, how those records were used, and their relationships to other sources. The variety of media on which these records are found changes along with improvements in technology and now include films, video and sound recordings, computer tapes, and video and optical disks. Archivists also have duties relating to administration, management, training, marketing, and public relations.

Registrars

A strong computer background will be important for today's museum registrar. This position is charged with creating and maintaining records for all objects that both enter and leave the collection. Museum registrars assign record numbers; complete accession sheets; number objects; assist in packing, unpacking, and shipping of loan objects; maintain donor forms; and complete computer records on all objects. They must be well versed in handling and storage techniques and have significant computer skills, including database management and spreadsheet familiarity.

Preparators

The preparator is responsible for installing and disassembling exhibits. They plan and direct fabrication, installation, and disassembly of both permanent and temporary museum exhibits. In addition, they administer budgets, personnel, and operations of their department. The chief preparator reports directly to the chief curator or director of the facility.

Directors/Administrators

Museums, collections, galleries, historic homes, and outdoor sites all need experienced administrators to act as chief operating officers, administering the budget, overseeing programming, collections and exhibits, implementing and initiating a strong development program, directing planning activities, supervising staff, and representing the institution to outside publics.

The history graduate very often doesn't think of curator/archivist positions as an employment opportunity following graduation. Hopefully, the discussion in this career path will lead you to take a serious look at the wonderful careers in these fields that will make use of and build upon your history degree and, more importantly, the curiosity and fascination with the past that led you to your degree in the first place. But, just as you might not have thought much about these kinds of jobs, you probably haven't been exposed to many job advertisements for curatorial/archival positions. We've tried to include several throughout our discussion to illustrate some points.

Working Conditions

The world of curators and archivists is as diverse as your interests. A good demonstration of the variety that exists is contained in the following ads.

> **Site Manager.** Seventeenth-century historic house. Duties include PR, grant writing, volunteer development, advancement of educational/curatorial goals. Requires related B.A., computer skills. Résumé and letter . . .

> **Assistant Curator.** Archival program includes local records, mss, and genealogical material. Continue program, reduce backlog, develop further, help with museum operations. Requires knowledge of all phases of archival work, prefer photo lab and computer background. Résumé and letter to . . .

Textiles, eighteenth-century decorative arts and furnishings, or archival work with special emphasis on photography—take your choice—are just a few examples of the diversity of focus possible in the fields of curatorial and archival work. Tremendous interest, excitement, and even love of your chosen field are important as the principal working conditions. If you don't find your subject endlessly fascinating, it will be difficult to sustain the drive, energy, and creativity needed to forge a career.

Beyond your subject area for curating or archiving, there are other areas of responsibility common to more experienced individuals working in these fields, regardless of the type of institution or nature of the collection or presentation.

Administration
A variety of other staff, including custodial, managerial, research, and technical will oversee and manage. There are also policies and procedures to write and administer, and significant correspondence to originate and respond to. In addition, budget preparation is a crucial task.

Working with Volunteers
Many historic sites, museums, galleries, installations, gardens, herbariums, zoos, and historic sites employ significant numbers of skilled volunteers who require training, scheduling, observation, and evaluation.

Raising Money
Curators and archivists may not have principal charge of raising funds but often are called upon to share in the development activities of their employer. This may mean attendance at social functions, briefing potential donors on the work of the organization, writing letters, or making fund-raising telephone calls to solicit donations.

Planning/Implementing/Acquisitions/Collection Changes
Always on the lookout for an opportunity to fill a gap or trade some item for something more desirable, curators and archivists must constantly stay abreast of other collections and items that may be available for purchase or trade. This requires attendance at conferences, visits to other installations, correspondence, and a significant time commitment to networking.

Researching
Extensive research is required to best display, maintain, and educate visitors about any collection. As new research is uncovered, documentation likewise needs to be updated. Research is an ongoing task of the curator/archivist.

Training and Qualifications

We hope you have found it gratifying to read many of the job announcements cited in this chapter and discover that the requisite qualification is a history degree. That, in fact, is your primary qualification. However, there are history degrees and there are history degrees. The assumption in requiring a major in history by the employer is that you know history; that you have a solid grasp of history in general and, hopefully, a more refined sense of some specific area of history (the first freed slaves in America, the Canadian fishing industry, the development of railroads during the nineteenth century, and so forth).

You will be expected to write and speak effectively. If there is one strong message throughout this chapter, it is that these positions in curatorship and archives management are public oriented and information brokers. You need to be comfortable interacting with diverse publics and communicating effectively in person or through scholarly articles, correspondence with members, even solicitations for development funds.

Organizational ability in managing your collection, supervising staff, and structuring time for administration and research and all of the behind-the-scenes support work of any collection is an important quality. In fact, many curators and archivists frequently cite maintaining the delicate balance between keeping themselves and the collections available to their publics for information purposes and the need to secure time for writing and research as a constant struggle.

Artifacts, prints, books, paintings, even buildings need records, identification, numbering, histories, and countless other details recorded and maintained. All of this information needs to be available to meet numerous requests. How much did you spend on acquisitions this year? What was the average purchase amount? How many volunteer hours was the collection given by volunteer staff, and who did the most? How many items are on loan to other institutions? You can easily see that without strong computer skills, especially database management and spreadsheet software familiarity, your job would be an impossible task.

Interns

The beginning of many careers, an internship is really an opportunity to explore, to observe, and, quite frankly, to make mistakes. Once in a while, the authors will have one of their career clients return from an internship vowing, "I'll never do that for a living!" That's OK, in fact, that's a valuable lesson learned with very little risk. It's much better to take an internship for little or no money and a limited time period and learn you don't like the job than to seek career employment and all the changes that go with it only to be unhappy.

Internships that expose workers to all aspects of museum programming, administration, and operations make for the best experiences. One source of information about internships is Employment Resources Online (employment-resources.com). Organizations such as the National Archives and Records

Administration (nara.gov) often post internship information. Also visit the websites of potential employers to determine if they offer internships. Many such sites describe internship opportunities you may be interested in exploring.

The work you do will help highlight your skills and abilities and allow you to demonstrate and display those talents to others. The people you might meet during these experiences will also prove helpful as you network for job opportunities. Your direct supervisors in these intern or volunteer experiences will also be able to provide the most specific references for any future jobs in the curator/archivist role.

Earnings

You'll notice that none of the job notices cited in this chapter includes salary information. Earnings of curators and archivists are impacted by several factors, including the type of organization (for-profit versus nonprofit), the size of the organization, the size of the collection, the perceived importance of the collection, and the region of the country where the collection is held. According to the U.S. Department of Labor, the median income for archivists was slightly more than $36,000 annually in 2004. Some experienced archivists earn more than $60,000 per year. Those employed as museum curators by the federal government earned over $76,000 yearly in 2005.

Networking with professionals who are employed at the type of organization where you hope to work is your best bet. These people will be able to provide the most up-to-date salary information available. Don't overlook this important information source.

Career Outlook

Thousands of museums, exhibit areas, collections, libraries, nature centers, and zoos operate in the United States and Canada today. They collect, display, and explain art, science, history, natural history, and other special subjects for the public. All these sites need workers. Thousands of people are employed either full-time or part-time, and tens of thousands of volunteers help them to do their job.

Archivists and curators are considered professional specialty workers, and the U.S. Department of Labor, Bureau of Labor Statistics indicates that this category of worker will increase about as fast as the average for all occupations through 2014. Three factors affect this growth: (1) continuing public interest in science, history, art, and technology, leading to the establishment of new facilities; (2) historically low turnover in these occupations; and (3) expected retirements.

Competition is keen for archival and curatorial positions even though new facilities are opening and baby boomers are nearing retirement. Those who enter these fields of work are not as likely to shift careers. If you take the steps outlined in the following section, Strategies for Finding the Jobs, you'll be well on your way to being considered a viable candidate for the positions you seek.

Strategies for Finding the Jobs

Directly related college course work and work experience are essential for success in a job search for someone interested in curatorial or archival work. Your strategy must include the following: incorporating at least one internship into your work history, taking any related courses (museum studies, information management) offered at your college or university, finding out about issues and problems professionals are currently facing, preparing yourself to apply for and accept preprofessional technical or entry-level positions, and considering graduate study so that you can advance your career in this field.

Incorporate at Least One Internship into Your Work History
Nearly every job listing, whether it is for part-time, seasonal, or full-time work, indicates that the position requires some level of experience. So how can you get experience if no one will hire you without it? In short, the practicum or internship. In a best-case scenario, you should plan on doing an internship in both your junior and senior years to be able to list relevant experience on your résumé. Employment Resources Online (employment-resources.com) is a good source for current listings through its "Internship Help Center." The website of the National Archives and Records Administration (nara.gov) posts internship openings around the country. And don't forget to contact museums you may be interested in working for to find out about their internship programs.

Take Museum Studies Courses If They Are Offered at Your College or University
A large group of people are attracted to the kind of work done in museum settings. And remember, you'll be competing for entry-level jobs against candidates who have actually majored in museum or library studies. So take advantage of any type of related course work offered at your institution. Also

look for workshops offered by professional associations or organizations or museums themselves. Review the last part of this chapter for association contact information.

Find Out About Current Issues and Problems

Browse the many websites listed in this chapter, glance at a current issue of *The American Archivist*, read through the online bookstore catalog of the American Association of Museums, or browse the Canadian Museums Association site (museum.ca), and you'll realize the range of issues that these professions face today. From understanding your audience to removing barriers for people with disabilities, or improving environmental protection of collections and facility security, all are important to working professionals. Keep up on the latest concerns and trends by reading professional journals. At the end of this chapter we have listed a number of professional associations and publications they make available. Some websites will allow you to access selected articles and information. College and university libraries and larger public libraries will carry some of these. Begin reading as many publications and journals as you have time for; it will be time well spent as you prepare your résumé and get ready to meaningfully answer tough interview questions.

Be Ready to Take Preprofessional Entry-Level Jobs If You Don't Have a Master's Degree

Because curatorial and archival work require a high level of specialization, the entry-level positions will be called, in some cases, internships, or might have the label of "technician." Read each advertisement carefully and apply for each job that you're qualified for, no matter what it's called. This will be a building block for moving on to higher-level positions that have the title "curator" or "archivist" but that also require more expertise.

Plan on Attending Graduate School If You Want Career Advancement

A variety of entry-level positions for history majors who have taken related course work and who have completed an internship are available, but additional academic training and experience are required to move beyond these positions. If your career interests lie in curatorial or archival work, be sure to explore graduate school options. With the assistance of a career counselor or librarian, use resources such as the graduate planner offered by Peterson's (petersons.com) to identify appropriate graduate programs. Network with administrators of local museums to seek their advice on graduate programs that they feel qualify a worker for positions beyond those at the entry level.

Possible Employers

As you are considering employment sites for curatorial and archival work, be sure to include:

Colleges and universities
Corporations
Museums, botanical gardens, and zoos
National, state, and local governments
Nonprofit organizations

Each will offer employment opportunities, and your search should include investigation of each type of site.

Museums, Botanical Gardens, and Zoos

There are more than seven thousand museums of various types that are members of the American Association of Museums (aam-us.org). Fourteen categories of institutions have been defined by the Association, and they include:

Art museums
Children's junior museums
College and university museums
Company museums
Exhibit areas
General museums (art and history)
History museums (maritime, military, and naval)
Libraries with collections of books
Libraries with collections other than books
National and state agencies, councils, and commissions
Nature centers
Park museums and visitor centers
Science museums (zoo, natural history, and aquarium)
Specialized museums

Those organizations classified as art museums include art associations, councils and commissions, foundations and institutes; art museums and galleries; arts and crafts museums; china, glass, and silver museums; civic art and cultural centers; decorative arts museums; folk art museums; and textile museums.

History museums have also been subcategorized: historic agencies, councils, commissions, foundations, and research institutes; historic houses and historic buildings; historic sites; historical and preservation societies; historical society museums; history museums; maritime/naval museums and historic ships; military museums; and preservation projects.

Museums falling into the science category can be any one of the following: academies, associations, institutes, and foundations; aeronautics and space museums; anthropology and ethnology museums; aquariums, marine museums, and oceanariums; arboretums; archaeology museums and archaeological sites; aviaries and ornithology museums; botanical and aquatic gardens, conservatories, and horticultural societies; entomology museums; geology, mineralogy, and paleontology museums; herbariums; herpetology museums; medical, dental, health, pharmacology, apothecary, and psychiatry museums; natural history and natural science museums; planetariums, observatories, and astronomy museums; science museums and centers; wildlife refuges and bird sanctuaries; and zoos.

As you can tell from the names, specialized museums are categorized by the specific type of collection they house. These museums specialize in agriculture, antiques, architecture, audiovisual and film, circus, comedy, communications, costume, crime, electricity, fire fighting, forestry, furniture, gun, hobby, horology, industry, lapidary arts, logging and lumber, maps, mining, money and numismatics, musical instruments, philately, photography, religion, scouting, sports, technology, theater, toys and dolls, transportation, typography, village, wax, whaling, and woodcarving.

Help in Locating These Employers. *The Official Museum Directory* (officialmuseumdirectory.com) and the *American Art Directory* (american artdir.com), both published by National Register, can be used to help you locate these organizations by type of museum or by geographic location. Several other websites are also very helpful including the International Council of Museums' site (icom.org), which contains a global registry of museum website addresses, and the Museum Register (museumregister.com), which links users to selected museums. Other good resources are available, both in book form and on the Web, so don't limit your search to these few references.

Nonprofit Organizations

Nonprofits hiring curators and/or archivists can range from conservation organizations, to religious and fraternal organizations, to professional associations. If a nonprofit organization has a prized collection, a library, or historical records, they'll want qualified employees to care for these resources.

Help in Locating These Employers. Finding out about all of the potential nonprofit employers will take some research on your part. Information about more than 1.5 million nonprofit organizations is available on a website developed for donors, but you may find it very useful, too. GuideStar's site (guidestar.org) allows you to locate nonprofits in a particular state or by a keyword. Actual job listings are not provided, but you will find useful information about the organizations, including addresses and telephone numbers. There are many similar sites. Just use your favorite search engine and enter the words *nonprofit organizations*, and you'll get lots of hits.

Your area's chamber of commerce may be aware of a local or regional directory of nonprofits you could utilize to locate these organizations. In addition, some regional or statewide business journals or newspapers occasionally highlight the nonprofit organizations functioning in the geographic region they cover. Check your school's career library or the local public library for copies of these types of publications.

Colleges and Universities
About one-sixth of all archivists and curators are employed by colleges and universities. Some teach or work in the institution's libraries. Many colleges and universities also have their own museums, which may house various types of collections including natural history, visual arts, and anthropological or geologic specimens. These campus museums are often an integral component of the academic and cultural mission of the institution. Curators who work here usually also take on teaching duties.

Help in Locating These Employers. If you are looking for actual job listings for colleges and universities, you will want to examine *The Chronicle of Higher Education* (chronicle.com), which lists jobs in the United States, Canada, and some other nations. *The Official Museum Directory* will help those of you interested in undertaking proactive networking to determine where most of these museums are located. You could also use Peterson's website (petersons.com) to identify schools that offer a degree in museum studies; usually, they will also house a museum.

National, State, and Local Governments
Federal, state, and local governments continue to be the largest employers in this country, and approximately one-third of all archivists and curators work in governmental positions. In terms of federal workers, most archivists are employed by the National Archives and Records Administration (nara.gov) or the Department of Defense (defenselink.mil). Curators work primarily for

the Smithsonian Institution (si.edu), in Defense Department military museums, or in other museums under the direction of the Department of the Interior (doi.gov). Canadian employers in this sector include the Canadian Council for the Arts (canadacouncil.ca) and the Canadian War Museum (warmuseum.ca).

The National Archives has custody of the permanent records of the federal government, with holdings dating from 1789 to the present. The mission of this office is to arrange and describe the records, preserve them, and make them available to the public for research. In the Washington area there are various archival units, including The National Archives Building, Washington, D.C.; the National Archives at College Park, Maryland; the Federal Register, Washington, D.C.; and the Washington National Records Center.

Conservators, museum curators, and museum technicians are employed by the Smithsonian Institution (si.edu). The Smithsonian is made up of almost twenty museums including the National Zoological Park, the National Portrait Gallery, and the National Air and Space Museum. The Smithsonian also includes the National Gallery of Art (nga.gov), the Woodrow Wilson International Center for Scholars (http://wwics.si.edu), and the John F. Kennedy Center for the Performing Arts (kennedy-center.org). Generally, turnover at the Smithsonian is quite low, because the organization tries to fill higher-level positions by promoting current employees. Openings tend to occur in entry-level positions vacated because of promotion. As with many government jobs, tenacity will be one of your most important job-seeking traits.

State governments also maintain historical records and run museums and libraries, and so have a need to hire archivists and curators. Other state agencies, including libraries, museums, parks, and zoos, hire curators.

Help in Locating These Employers. If you are interested in exploring opportunities available with the Office of the National Archives, visit their website (nara.gov) or contact one of the regional offices listed at the end of this chapter to get the latest information on hiring needs and procedures.

The Smithsonian Institution is included on a list of federal departments and agencies that employ the great majority of federal workers. Contact the Institution in Washington, D.C., via Internet or phone for current hiring information.

If you would like to review information about federal employment, visit the Office of Personnel Management's website (usajobs.opm.gov). For state government positions, explore the state's websites or look in the yellow pages for the telephone number of a local or regional state employment office. For local government positions you can try the Internet or contact the government directly and ask how to find out about current job openings. Many government agencies, both state and local, have recorded job listings available by calling a special number. These numbers are well advertised. McGraw-Hill publishes a career guide titled *Opportunities in Government Careers* that provides information important to your job search.

Corporations

Large corporations with record centers often employ archivists to oversee records management. Certain information provides a strategic advantage to the organization and must be carefully organized, protected, and made accessible to those employees who are authorized to use it. Some organizations also house museums, including Eli Lilly and Company, Coca-Cola, Corning, Boeing, and Dupont. Research organizations also hire archivists to manage the data and information that keep them in business.

Help in Locating These Employers. Two publications you can use to begin identifying possible employers are the *Official Museum Directory* and the *Research Centers and Services Directory*. Work with a career counselor or librarian to identify other references that will be useful for your job search.

Possible Job Titles

Curator and archivist are familiar titles, but have you also considered fine arts packer or museum technician as you read through job listings and newsletters? Review the entire list shown here and consider jobs that are given these other labels. Add to the list; you'll see other titles not shown here. Don't let names fool you. Read the qualifications to see if you should apply.

Archivist
Art conservator
Artifacts conservator
Assistant curator
Assistant director, museum
Associate curator
Associate director for historic resources
Ceramic restorer
Collections manager
Curator
Curator of collections
Curatorial associate

Fine arts packer
Lace and textiles restorer
Manager
Museum curator
Museum technician
Paper conservator
Site administrator
Site manager

Related Occupations

Think about what curators and archivists do: they are historians, teachers, guides, explorers, and impresarios. They are thought of as artistic, enterprising, and social. There are other jobs and career choices that draw on a combination of some of these, as well as other skills and abilities. Have you also thought about these?

Arborist
Art director
Assistant registrar
Botanist
Decorator
Folklorist
Graphic designer
Information specialist
Interior decorator
Librarian
Lighting designer
Marketing director
Museum registrar
Museum sales manager
Preparator
Public information director
Publications editor
Records manager
Sales representative
Volunteer coordinator

Be sure to read up on those positions that sound interesting but that you don't know as much about. See the *Occupational Outlook Handbook* (bls.gov/oco) for the additional information you might need.

Professional Associations

Because curators and archivists must, for the most part, specialize in a field of study, associations for specific types of museums and organizations are shown below. Contact, or possibly join, those that offer services or products you need.

American Association of Museums
1575 I St. NW, Suite 400
Washington, DC 20005
aam-us.org
Members/Purpose: Art, history, and science museums; art associations and centers; historic houses and societies; preservation projects; planetariums; zoos; aquariums; botanical gardens; college and university museums; and others interested in the museum field.
Journals/Publications: *Aviso*; *Museum News*; *jobHQ* (formerly *Aviso Museum Careers*)
Job Listings: Maintains placement services for museum professionals; see *Aviso* for employment opportunities in museums.

American Institute for Conservation of Historical and Artistic Works
1717 K St. NW, Suite 200
Washington, DC 20036
aic.stanford.edu
Members/Purpose: Professionals, scientists, administrators, educators, and others interested in the field of art conservation; seeks to advance knowledge and improve methods of conservation needed to protect, preserve, and maintain the condition and integrity of objects or structures that because of their history, significance, rarity, or workmanship have a commonly accepted value and importance for the public interest.
Training: Conducts seminars and lectures.
Journals/Publications: *AIC News*; *Journal of the American Institute for Conservation*
Job Listings: See *AIC News*.

Association of African American Museums
P.O. Box 578
Wilberforce, OH 45384
blackmuseums.org
Members/Purpose: Museums, museum professionals, and scholars concerned with preserving, restoring, collecting, and exhibiting African-American history and culture.

Training: Conducts professional training workshops.
Journals/Publications: *African American Heritage Directory*; newsletters
Job Listings: Provides job listings for members.

Association of College and University Museums and Galleries
Ursinus College
601 East Main St.
Collegeville, PA 19426
Members/Purpose: Institutions and individuals professionally involved with college and university museums and galleries.
Training: None
Journal/Publication: *News and Issues* newsletter
Job Listings: None

Association of Railway Museums
P.O. Box 370
Tujunga, CA 91043-0370
railwaymuseums.org
Members/Purpose: Organizations having as their entire or partial purpose the preservation of railway equipment, artifacts, and history.
Training: None
Journal/Publication: *Railway Museum Quarterly*
Job Listings: None

Canadian Association of Science Centres (CASC)
c/o Canadian Museum of Nature
P.O. Box 3443, Station D
Ottawa, ON K1P 6P4
canadiansciencecentres.ca
Members/Purpose: Promotes cooperation among Canada's science centres and works to provide a single voice before government.
Training: Annual general meetings and other opportunities.
Journals/Publications: Members' directory; quarterly newsletter; research publications
Job Listings: None

The Canadian Museums Association
280 Metcalfe St., Suite 400
Ottawa, ON K2P 1R7
museums.ca
Members/Purpose: Represents Canadian museum professionals both within Canada and internationally in nonprofit museums, art galleries,

science centres, aquaria, archives, sport halls of fame, artist-run centres, zoos, and historic sites; works for the recognition, growth, and stability of the sector while serving nearly two thousand members by providing training and professional development programs, conferences, publications, networking opportunities and relevant information.

Training: Offers annual national conference, museum shop conferences, regional symposiums, workshops, and training resources.

Journals/Publications: *Muse* magazine; news alerts; member directory

Job Listings: Offers online jobs board.

International Sports Heritage Association

P.O. Drawer 3093
Ponte Vedra Beach, FL 32004
sportshalls.com

Members/Purpose: Seeks to improve and maintain standards of sports museums and halls of fame and enhance their operations; facilitates the exchange of information; institutes projects that may be useful to all members.

Training: None

Journals/Publications: *ISHAE Newsletter*; *Honoring Our Heroes*; membership directory

Job Listings: None

National Foundation for Jewish Culture

330 Seventh Ave., 21st Floor
New York, NY 10001
jewishculture.org

Members/Purpose: Jewish museums, historical societies, and nonprofit galleries united to support, encourage, and promote the development of American Jewish museums in collecting, preserving, and interpreting Jewish art and artifacts for public education and the advancement of scholarship.

Training: None

Journals/Publications: *Jewish Culture News*; newsletters; research reports

Job Listings: None

Shaker Museum and Library

88 Shaker Museum Rd.
Old Chatham, NY 12136
shakermuseumandlibrary.org

Members/Purpose: To preserve and interpret the arts, skills, philosophy, and economic-cultural contributions of the United Society of Believers in Christs' Second Appearing (Shakers).
Training: None
Journal/Publication: *Broadside*
Job Listings: None

Society of American Archivists
527 S. Wells St., 5th Floor
Chicago, IL 60607
archivists.org
Members/Purpose: Professional association of individuals and institutions concerned with management of current records, archival administration, and the custody of historical manuscripts in government, business, and semipublic institutions.
Training: Conducts seminars and workshops.
Journals/Publications: *American Archivist Journal*; *Archival Outlook* newsletter; directory of individual members
Job Listings: SAA Employment Bulletin; online job listings.

United States Lighthouse Society
244 Kearny St., 5th Floor
San Francisco, CA 94108
uslhs.org
Members/Purpose: Promotes restoration and preservation of America's lighthouses.
Training: None
Journals/Publications: *Bulletin*; *The Keepers Log* magazine
Job Listings: None

8

Path 3: Information Specialization

Improvements in technology have accelerated not only the quantity and detail of information but the speed at which we can provide information to those needing it. Increasingly user-friendly computers, mp3 players, cell phones that double as personal digital assistants, the Internet, interactive television, facsimile machines, CD-ROMs, and a host of other devices have us swimming (some would say drowning) in information.

How do we manage it all? Can someone manage it for us? How can we select what is best and eliminate the rest? More important, how can we go back and retrieve something we read, saw, or heard and need right now?

A library is an excellent example of the need for information specialists. It also serves as an analogy for the work and role of the information specialist in any organization. A library, especially a large collection, is almost useless without the order imposed on it by indexing, cataloguing, shelving, and retrieval systems. Online catalogs provide the user with a book's location and availability. Without the system created by librarians (a type of information specialist), a library would be chaotic and of very little use to us despite its potential.

But librarians do more than just order and shelve their collections. They create systems for sharing material with users and between collections. Interlibrary loans are a good example of information specialists' ability to provide what they don't have by establishing sharing networks with those that do. Consortiums of libraries often share databases and allow us to search the catalogs of other collections for material or references we may require.

In a nutshell, the mission of the information specialist is to connect the information seeker with the desired information. Written out, it seems a simple mission. But it is far more complex a task to accomplish than it is to express, and it will call upon all of the history graduate's skills to perform this job with efficiency, frequently under time and cost constraints, and with the degree of specificity sought by the information requester.

Here's an ad that really emphasizes thoroughness, specificity, and follow-through in a profit-oriented business:

IT Resource Director. Solid company seeks a qualified individual to manage a staff of 25 people who build and produce the data that support the company's product line. Successful applicant must be able to maintain product categories that are kept up to date with the fast-paced computer industry. All information must be accurate and thorough. All products must have complete descriptions that enable online customers to select, with ease, the correct item the first time. Close attention must be paid to new and changing product lines, upgrades, versions, and discounted products. You will be responsible for continually finding new and better ways to productively manage large amounts of information.

This position is an outstanding opportunity for a highly motivated individual who has strong skills in directing people toward productivity issues as well as communicate clearly with management and customers.

The information specialist must master a number of important skills in addition to his or her content area. Many of these skills, however, will have been practiced and used in your study of history and will prove equally valuable in a career in information management. Let's identify and analyze some of these skills.

- **Content mastery.** Knowledge of a subject is the touchstone of the information specialist. If, for example, you begin working for a company that manufactures eyeglasses and eye care products, you would soon learn that glasses are considered by many as more than just vision aids, but also as a complementary product to clothing or even as a kind of fashion statement in themselves. As changes take place in the world of fashion, the eye care industry must follow suit (or at least take them into consideration when developing new products. The initiatives of competing companies will also enter into the equation. Available frame colors and styles, the size and configuration of lenses, and other considerations will be important. To be a content expert in eye care products would mean having significant current information on trends in the overall fashion market, as well.

- **Needs assessment.** Don't expect everyone who requests information resources from you to be equally articulate about what he or she wants. One of your principal tasks will be to understand exactly what your clients need regardless of how they express it. Skillful questioning, clarification, and the ability to produce examples will help you and your clients come to agreement on exactly what is needed.

• **Instructing/mentoring.** An old, often-stated Chinese adage states: If you give a man a fish, you feed him for a day; if you teach a man how to fish, you feed him for life. This is particularly appropriate in the retrieval of information. Your job may be to provide the information requested, but there is no reason to keep your client in the dark about how that information was found and accessed. Every client you meet will benefit from your modeling and teaching your search activities to them so they can begin to understand how to mount their own search. You'll want to both help clients with their immediate needs and convey to them, at the same time, the excitement and pleasure of working on their own.

• **Networking.** Think of the information specialist not as a "keeper" of information but as a "finder." Certainly, in any stable employment situation, the individuals charged with information resourcing will build some files of their own. But they will never be able to acquire all they need. The information specialist doesn't necessarily amass information and then distribute it as requested. He or she often may have to generate the information needed within an organization and through the combined efforts of many departments. In providing a historical analysis of a company's billboard advertising over the past fifteen years to determine trends in outdoor advertising, you may first seek data from the marketing or public relations division, and also perhaps from branch offices of your company. You may do some research outside the organization on competitors' billboard strategies and employ the services of a librarian or commercial data retrieval firm. You may go on the Internet to locate information about the subject. Very often your work is the product of cooperation among many individuals, and information specialists maintain elaborate and well-developed networks of contacts to provide them the information they need.

• **Juggling.** Often, you won't have the luxury of working on one information request by itself, from initial request through to delivery. More often, you'll juggle the requests of many individuals simultaneously. Some of these requests will be complicated and involve significant research and accumulation of materials that involve time delays. Some may involve mailings and phone calls to acquire the needed answers. Because some of your work depends on others, you will find yourself working on many, many projects simultaneously.

Excellent organizational skills, time-management ability, and a tolerance for stress will ease the challenges of keeping so many requests and searches going at the same time.

Definition of the Career Path

The introduction to this career path may have helped explain the need for information specialists. We have described how, in today's fast-paced, information-oriented society, our need may be not for information but for someone to extract what we need from an overwhelming oversupply. Most of us frequently have that need in our daily lives. Likewise, you can appreciate the skills and talents necessary for information specialists to be effective in their job. But what are those jobs and what are they called? Let's look at a short list of possible job titles:

Administrative assistant
Assistant editor
Assistant planner
Biographer
Communications assistant
Database/records manager
Development associate for research
Government relations assistant
Genealogist
Historian
Information specialist
Institutional researcher
Intelligence specialist
Library and information specialist
List and segmentation manager
Market researcher
Media specialist
Photograph cataloger
Records information manager
Registrar
Research analyst
Systems manager

The variety and confusion of working titles should indicate several important things to the job searcher. First, the field of information specialization remains largely undefined, at least in job titles. Certainly, those who employ people to act as information specialists have not yet agreed on a common terminology. The lack of a definitive job title may also indicate individual job roles vary equally as much. People working in informational services are still organizing themselves by content area and not by their more general role as information networkers. Second, the lack of a common job title requires you to read and carefully understand the job description for which you are applying. It is in these job duties and the delineations of responsibility that you will come to appreciate the focus and emphasis in that particular position and not only whether it meets your expectations of the job of an information specialist, but also if you have the particular skill package the employer is seeking.

Look at the variety of position descriptions shown below to begin to gain additional insight into the work of the information specialist:

HR Research Assistant. Do you have a knack for mining the Internet? (Major insurance company) needs effective research assistant to support HR recruiting/staffing function. Responsible for using advanced Internet search skills to mine the net to find candidates for internal, non-IT positions. Must have a bachelor's degree, be Internet savvy, have some experience researching, and have great organizational and communications skills. Flexible schedules considered. Competitive wages and benefits. Send information to …

Information Technician. (Pharmaceutical manufacturer) seeking information specialist in company's research library. Assist corporate librarian with all functions and work on an array of research projects in support of all operations. Must be highly proficient in MS Office, provide exceptional customer service and accurate results, be an independent worker/thinker, and possess patience. Bachelor's degree required, library experience helpful, training or experience in chemistry, biology, or biotechnology a plus.

Information Technologist. (Large private foundation) working on an international document imaging and scanning project. Help organize and implement an information system. B.A./B.S. required. Possession of organizational and verbal/written communication skills; library, archives, records management, and customer service a plus. Highly competitive salary and comprehensive health plan.

Associate Web Editor. (East Coast merchandiser) has an immediate opening for an associate Web editor. Major duties: identify, screen, evaluate, and choose sites to link to corporate website; categorize sites by currency and content, write descriptions of sites; write and edit new materials for corporate website; coordinate assignments for freelance writers; work with search engine company; work with editor to coordinate with reviews and features; work with book team as needed to maintain books database. Minimum of a bachelor's degree in a related field, extensive experience with Web writing and design, and polished writing and editing skills.

Working Conditions

Get ready to be popular and busy. The woman or man who can provide on-target information when it's needed is going to be a vital member of any organization. In an information specialist position, you have the opportunity to meet with coworkers from every department and level of employment within your organization. You'll be called on frequently, not just for formal requests for information, but also with simple questions such as, "How many workers did we have in 1990?" or "Where exactly in the city was our first showroom?" The information resource professional is very often (and wisely) brought in early in the planning stages of most projects so they have a full understanding of the information needs of all concerned parties. This helps them to best consider how to accomplish the task.

Involvement

High-level involvement may come as a surprise to some who are unaware of the active role information specialists play not only in providing data support to planning needs but in helping to shape strategy. Knowledge of the organization's past experiences, successes, and failures and an ability to bring those experiences to bear on new efforts make the information specialist a player and not just a resource.

Communication

Listening, questioning, and determining needs are vital skills, and the information resource specialist needs to interact with people constantly to best ascertain what information. Your possession of strong interpersonal skills will help you work quicker and smarter if you can communicate successfully, using an easy-to-understand vocabulary and visual aids to gain an understanding of what information people need.

Working conditions will involve lots of partnerships and cooperation with others in a variety of fields. Your networks of contacts will be vital and your day will include much telephone and computer work and probably a fair amount of written correspondence. The information specialist is far more of a communicator than a bookworm.

Quick Action

You may be surprised to hear speed mentioned in a research job. A common complaint of the information specialist is "everybody wants it yesterday." Fortunately, many requests repeat themselves with stunning regularity, and the skillful resource professional will begin to build information packets to satisfy those traditional requests. But many searches are challenging and are prompted by a need to respond to some outside influence or market demand quickly. If you begin with a clear and mutually agreed-upon definition of the materials and information requested, you have accomplished the most important element in rapid information provision. Good staff, technology, a strong memory, note-taking ability, records management, and retrieval will all help you to get information seekers what they need as quickly as possible.

Tracking and Traffic Management

Stop in at a busy information specialist's office, and somewhere, on a desk, on the wall, on the computer screen, you're likely to discover a tracking chart of all the various ongoing projects and their individual stages of completion. Seldom does one have the luxury of a single project; there are usually many. The atmosphere may not be exactly chaotic, but it won't remind you of the traditional image of the library. It might be closer to the newsroom of a major daily before it goes to press. The reason for this is interesting and informative about the profession. You may well ask, "Why not just work straight through on one assignment, finish it, and move on to the next?" It's a reasonable question and has an interesting answer.

Frequently, the information specialist cannot immediately acquire the materials or data she or he needs and must seek the help of another information specialist to provide that. This may involve letters, facsimile transmissions, electronic mail, or telephone calls anywhere in the world. There will be delays as these individuals have their own agenda of tasks and they, in turn, may need to seek out additional information! Keeping track of these requests and the projects they relate to can be a task in itself. There is even a name for it: traffic management!

Training and Qualifications

All information specialists have their own combinations of skills and attributes and each brings something special to the job. Information resourcing can involve great creativity, intuition, and educated guesswork. Those are hard to determine in the interview process and even harder to pin down and evaluate. There are several attributes that go into the skill package of the information specialist, and though how they are prioritized might be the subject of intense debate, most would agree on the following basic list.

Organization

Every part of your job in information management cries for organization. Organizing your resources, your time, and your priorities to fulfill the information requests you receive will make constant and ever-increasing demands on your organizational ability. How frustrating and wasteful to be asked for something you've done before and yet can no longer locate, necessitating an entire repeat search. In any self-assessment exercise, organization should be a strong personal quality for an information specialist.

Strong Computing Capability

Regardless of the exact position you are seeking, chances are that you'll need to be able to demonstrate that you possess strong computing capabilities. At a minimum, your skills should include the ability to use word processing software, spreadsheets, e-mail and Internet search techniques. Capabilities in Web design and desktop publishing can also be a great asset, as is familiarity with specialized databases. A basic knowledge of computing will allow you to connect the information seeker with the desired information quickly.

High Level of General Information

Knowing your content area seems obvious, whether it's sports merchandising, textbook publishing, or trends in the mortgage industry. Reading the daily newspaper, watching television, and keeping up with news magazines, literature, and other conduits of general information may be more critical. It is in how people speak, read, and write about the facts you are dealing with that will allow you to make the necessary important connections between seemingly unrelated topics. What if your inquiry required descriptions of architecture from eighteenth-century novels or a listing of those cityscapes most often used to back the credits of situation comedies?

Listening Skills and Needs Assessment

Frequently, you'll get requests for information that you don't understand. You know that to do the best job you can, you need to be of the same mind as the information requester. That person may be unused to dealing with an information specialist and not particularly adept at expressing his or her informational needs. That's where your communication skills come into play. Skillful questioning, a patient manner with good eye contact, and attending behavior will encourage people to express exactly what they perceive to be their request. Your questions and discussion will help clarify the request and bring your results closer to their original intention. You must be ready to do this with representatives from every department, every level of the employment hierarchy, or society in general.

Earnings

Webmaster, online researcher, editorial assistant, public relations specialist, information technician, data coordinator—the names for information specialist positions continue to grow. If you're interested in this field, which promises to continue to be an exciting and challenging one, then you probably already enjoy solving problems. Finding accurate earnings information may well be your first assignment!

To get a good handle on the possible earnings range or "spread" for an entry-level information specialist, you'll need to look at these positions (by whatever job title) across the full spectrum of possible employment sites (nonprofit, business/industry, education, libraries, and so forth). Government-position salaries may pay in the high-twenties to low thirties, or sometimes higher, for bachelor-degree holders with minimum experience. College and university positions (database management, library positions that don't require a master's degree) range somewhat higher. Research assistants in business and industry with solid software skills may earn in the mid- to high thirties, or sometimes higher, in their first position.

If you bring to your first position some specific information management experience, better-than-average computer skills, and strong documentation of these abilities, you can expect your entry-level salary to more closely approximate the high end of a stated range. For stated entry-level salaries, you may be able to negotiate as much as ten percent more with exceptional experience.

Career Outlook

The term "information overload" has real meaning for most of us in our personal lives. We have mailboxes full of junk mail, newspapers and magazines, incomprehensible numbers of software packages available for our home computer, lengthy recorded messages waiting for us on our voice mail, and satellite television access to hundreds of channels. How can we possibly manage such a plethora of information? We can't, and we don't have to manage this personal influx of data, because it is discretionary. We can choose where we put our time and energy and ignore information that doesn't interest us.

This is not the case, however, for business, medical, or educational institutions; governmental agencies; or any of the host of professional information receivers. The proliferation of databases, online services, print publications, and Internet services demands to be managed. Incoming material needs to be screened, selected, and stored for easy access and retrieval. For many of these professional sites, information access can mean important advantages in the cost of doing business, in maintaining a competitive edge, or in providing critical response to a consumer.

There are books written about data mining and websites for data miners. One consultant's site (dataminers.com) describes data mining as "one of the most exciting developments in the field of decision support. It is rapidly transforming the fields of retailing, cataloguing, database marketing, insurance, and financial services by allowing corporations to use their extensive stores of data to better understand customer behavior."

Given all of the information needs of our society, the outlook is a positive one. However, in any growing field, this demand for specialists will engender two other demands. First, hiring criteria will become increasingly demanding, so you'll want to stay competitive. This chapter has given you the information you need to make the most of your education and experience as you seek an entry-level position. Second, the technology in this industry will continue to develop and you must stay current in this area to stay marketable. Review the next section of this chapter to enhance your job search.

Strategies for Finding the Jobs

Information specialists can enhance their job search by incorporating the four considerations we describe into their efforts. Computers are becoming more important than ever in moving relevant information quickly, so it will be critical to get as much computer-related training as you can. In addition, you'll want to be sure to do some informational interviewing early on; you'll get the inside scoop on potential employers and the qualifications they are seeking. After you talk with these professionals you'll have a better sense for the kinds of information specialties that seem to match your interests and talents, and you'll want to follow that up by testing your decisions. As you do this testing in part-time employment or in internships, you'll have the opportunity to begin practicing the specialized skills you'll be called upon to use regularly. Each of these efforts will prepare you to move out into the world of work.

Get as Much Computer-Related Training as You Can

The movement from the use of paper records to the use of computerized records demands that the information specialist know how to use the latest technology, both in terms of hardware (computer terminals, personal computers, printers, scanners, digitizers) and software (word processing, databases, spreadsheets, telecommunications, graphics packages). Plan on taking courses or workshops that provide you with an overview of computers and technology as well as courses that provide hands-on training on specific types of software packages. Once you learn how to use one type of database or spreadsheet, you will be able to convince potential employers that it will be easy for you to learn the particular package they are using.

Do Some Informational Interviewing Early in Your Job Search

Informational interviewing will help you gather more information about jobs and work environments. Library work is often thought of as being solitary and in a very quiet setting. Talk with a professional to uncover the realities. Library staff members do have fun, and teamwork is critical to their success. Advertising is often thought of by students as a busy, hectic, and unconventional industry. Information specialists working in this industry may find themselves very busy indeed, but the work is often not as glamorous as some believe it is. No matter what type of work or work setting you are considering, find out what it's really like. Talk with other entry-level employees as well as seasoned veterans to get the complete picture so you can better judge for yourself whether that setting would be a "good place" to work.

Decide Which Specialization Interests You Most

To begin building a career as one of the types of information specialists described in this path, at a fairly early stage in your career you will have to make a decision about how you want to specialize. You will certainly be able to gain an entry-level position with a bachelor's degree, but to see career growth in an information specialty you will probably need an advanced degree. If library work interests you, for example, you would be able to obtain several types of library jobs with a bachelor's degree in history. If you hope to work as a librarian, a master's degree in library science will be required. Let's say you are interested in organizing the information gathered by a large corporation. An advanced degree in information systems management or a more general master's in business administration would be needed to move into upper levels of management.

So how do you begin deciding what to specialize in? Part-time work, summer jobs, and internships are all employment opportunities you can use while you're still in school to put yourself in various environments to see what they are like, to see what type of people work in these settings, and to gain a deeper understanding of the nature of the work.

One organization that offers a number of volunteer internship opportunities on an ongoing basis is the Student Conservation Association (thesca.org). A review of their website showed numerous opportunities that the information specialist might be interested in. For example, one position was for a historical researcher who would conduct research and gather oral histories on construction, history, and subsequent development of the Denali Highway in interior Alaska. Requirements included a major in history or a related field, self-motivation, ability to work independently and with minimal supervision, and the ability to work in remote areas with adverse environmental conditions.

If you have already graduated, you may want to consider temporary or term employment opportunities. This approach can be useful if you want to experience several types of jobs before you make a commitment to specialize in one area or field. There are temp agencies operating in nearly every geographic location, and some of them specialize in the type of placement they make (paralegal, systems management).

Begin Acquiring and Practicing the Necessary Specialized Skills

Most employers don't care whether you have built your skills in a classroom setting, in a part-time job or internship, or in a volunteer position. They just want to know that you'll be able to do the work they're hiring you to do. Having experience using needed skills will certainly set you apart from the group of people who simply say they *think* they can do the work. So get involved in using the computer or learning about a subject such as market research at every available opportunity.

Possible Employers

The information specialist will find employment opportunities lurking around every corner; your imagination may be the only factor limiting the possibilities you explore.

Consider these types of employers:

Business and industry
Consulting organizations
Government
Libraries
Nonprofit organizations
Research centers

Each is discussed below; be sure to add to the list as you do your own exploring.

Consulting Organizations

Consultants and consulting organizations help their clients, be they individuals or organizations, get information and solve problems. The issues can range from engineering to health care, from science and technology to pension funds. Consulting organizations with more than a few employees will have some type of information specialist on their staff. The work may involve library research, computer work, report writing, or sales presentations. Be ready to accept a job that allows you to get your foot in the door and then will allow you to grow once you show how effective you are.

Help in Locating These Employers. You can turn to a variety of sources when trying to locate the names of consulting organizations. Three helpful websites are offered by the Association of Professional Consultants (consultapc.org), Kennedy Information Consulting Central (consultingcentral.com), and (for an industry-specific example) the Canadian Telecommunications Consultants Association (ctca.ca). A directory you may find in your college's library is the *Consultants & Consulting Organizations Directory* published by Gale Group. Many more are available, so check with your career counselor or librarian for additional titles.

Research Centers

If you have enjoyed your academic experience and you like the idea of working in an academic community, a range of research centers, often affiliated with a college or university, provide the opportunity to work as an information specialist. Research centers might focus their work on agriculture, environmental sciences, medical issues, business, population and demography, folklore, labor and industrial relations, or nearly any other imaginable subject. Research centers hire many different types of employees, including library specialists, researchers, information systems managers, and survey managers. Identify possible employment sites by using the resources listed, and network with managers or directors of the facilities to find out about employment opportunities.

Help in Locating These Employers. Gale Group publishes two helpful directories that you may find in your career or college library. They are *International Research Centers Directory and Research Centers Directory*. Most universities house at least one research center, and the Internet will help you discover them. Use any search engine and enter the name of a well-known university near you and then search the site for research centers. In addition, most professional association sites on the Internet will connect you with an associated research facility.

Government

Information specialists can find employment at many different kinds of governmental agencies, which include state, provincial, and local planning departments; intelligence operations; regulatory agencies (for example nuclear power); city and town libraries; environmental protection agencies; law enforcement agencies; and housing and community development agencies.

U.S. and Canadian government agencies hire intelligence research specialists, program specialists, administrative assistants, historians, import specialists, management analysts, and position classification specialists, just to name a few possible titles. They work in agencies such as the National Archives, Drug Enforcement Administration, Canadian Human Rights Commission, Canadian Institutes of Health Research, Library and Archives Canada, National Endowment for the Humanities, National Park Service, National Research Council Canada, Smithsonian Institution, U.S. Customs Service, and the U.S. Information Agency.

State, provincial, and local governments offer positions in units including administration and legislation, corrections, court systems, education, fire protection, health and human services, highway and street construction and maintenance, housing and community development, hospitals, libraries, natural resources, parks and recreation, police, sanitation, transportation, and utilities. Many entry-level positions don't have the word "information" in the job title but are, in reality, information specialist positions.

Help in Locating These Employers. Government agencies worth checking into include National Archives (nara.gov), U.S. Department of Justice (usdoj.gov), National Endowment for the Humanities (neh.gov), National Research Council Canada (nrc-cnrc.gc.ca), Natural Resources Canada (nrcan rncan.gc.can), National Park Service (nps.gov), Smithsonian Institution (si.edu), U.S. Customs and Border Protection (customs.treas.gov), the Public Service Commission of Canada (psc-cfp.gc.ca), and the U.S. Information Agency (usia.gov). Their websites, as well as the Office of Personnel Management's site (usajobs.opm.gov) and Canadian sites such as All Canadian Jobs (allcanadianjobs.com) and Best Jobs Canada (bestjobsca.com) are your best sources for finding currently available government positions.

State governments and oftentimes local governments will have websites that list job openings. Check sites for states and cities where you are interested in working. Don't hesitate to ask for assistance in working through the application process. Remember, these personnel offices want to find capable and qualified employees to fill their positions.

Libraries

Libraries are often classified according to the populations they serve. These include school libraries; college, university, and research libraries; public libraries; and specialized or cooperative libraries. Each type of library has its own interests and faces its own challenges. School libraries, for example, are striving to improve their media centers, so one way to put to work your degree in history and your interest and part-time work experience in media operations is to seek employment as a media specialist in larger elementary and secondary schools.

Help in Locating These Employers. The American Library Association's website (ala.org) contains employment information as well as a link to their publication, *American Libraries.* Directories that you may find useful include the *American Library Directory* (americanlibrarydirectory.org), the *Directory of Special Libraries and Information Centers* (libraries-update.com), and *Directory of Libraries in Canada,* published by Canada Almanac and Directory. Another source of info is Libweb, a site providing links to library home pages in more than 130 countries including Canada and the United States (http://lists.webjunction.org.libweb). Also check the job listings in your local newspaper and on the Internet, or visit your career office to review specialized job listings they may subscribe to.

Business and Industry

We recently saw a job advertisement for an entry-level position with a large pharmaceutical company that we would classify as an information specialist. The position was called a marketing assistant, and the ad asked for someone who is smart and energetic for a range of functions, including telephone prospecting, Web research, file maintenance, word processing, and other support activities. They wanted a college degree with marketing exposure for a position that would provide new skills and opportunity to build a career. This calls for the information specialist! There are similar positions in advertising, information brokering, marketing research, financial services, information systems, and many other industries.

Help in Locating These Employers. Don't overlook using a business career resource such as McGraw-Hill's *Careers in Business*, which will orient you to the needs of the for-profit business community. You'll learn about the various industries and business functions, and the entry-level positions that they offer. Many are information specialists, in the sense that we have described here. Move on to more specific resources such as *100 Best Careers in Crime Fighting: Law Enforcement, Criminal Justice, Private Security, and Cyberspace Crime Detection*; *Pick Me: Breaking into Advertising and Staying There*; *Careers in High Tech*; or *Career Guide for the High Tech Professional*. These types of books will help you focus in on skills, abilities, and traits that you should highlight on your résumé and during the interview process.

Nonprofit Organizations

Whether you research donor prospects for a university, maintain a membership list for a large organization such as the American Bar Association, or coordinate volunteers for the American Cancer Society or Canadian Red Cross, you'll be using skills associated with being an information specialist. There are large, well-established nonprofit organizations that have proportionally as large a staff and run as efficiently as for-profit businesses and smaller, grassroots organizations that have only a few employees and have a very casual organizational culture. No matter what type of setting you prefer, these organizations must maintain information critical to their strategic advantage.

Help in Locating These Employers. Start with a review of *Career Opportunities in the Nonprofit Sector* or *Opportunities in Fund-Raising Careers* to get an overview of the scope and types of organizations that exist in this sector of the economy. Then move on to other resources, including *The Non-Profit Times*, the *Chronicle of Philanthropy*, and idealist.org. Reviewing two or three of these resources should help you determine whether the nonprofit sector is a place for you.

Possible Job Titles

As you look over the list of possible job titles you'll begin to realize there are innumerable job titles for you to consider, and many more titles could be added. As you conduct your job search, add to this list based on the job descriptions you read in advertisements and in other career guidebooks.

Administrative assistant
Assistant editor
Assistant planner
Bibliographer
Biographer
Classifier
Communications assistant
Corporate historian
Database network coordinator
Database/records manager
Development associate for research
Genealogist
Government relations assistant
Historian
Historic preservation planner
Historical researcher
Information hotline specialist
Information manager
Information scientist
Information specialist
Institutional researcher
Intelligence research specialist
Intelligence specialist
Librarian
Library and information specialist
Library circulation desk supervisor
Library reference coordinator
Library technical assistant
List and segmentation manager
Market researcher
Media specialist
Paralegal
Paralegal assistant
Photographic cataloger
Planner
Policy analyst
Registrar
Research analyst

Research assistant
Research associate
Research interviewer
Researcher
School librarian
Securities information researcher
Software specialist
Systems analyst
Systems manager
Technical research assistant
Travel agent

Related Occupations

Think about the roles played by an information specialist: content mastery, needs assessment, instructing/mentoring, nit-picking, networking, and multiple project juggling, and you'll see there are other career choices to consider if this one doesn't seem quite right. If you're not familiar with the job descriptions that go along with the job titles shown below, be sure to find out more about them. Consider:

Actuary
Admissions officer
Claims adjudicator
Computer programmer
Counselor
Curator
Customer service representative
Employment interviewer
Teacher

Use the *Occupational Outlook Handbook* in print or online (bls.gov.oco) to get a better idea of the nature of these jobs.

Professional Associations

In this section, we have listed a wide range of organizations that will be able to provide additional data about certain information specialties. Carefully review the Members/Purpose section for each organization and decide whether the organization pertains to your interests. Membership in one may well be worth the investment in terms of networking opportunities, job listings, or placement services. Remember, some organizations will provide limited career information at no charge, but if you want to receive publications that often include job listings, you must actually join the organization. Many do, however, have greatly reduced membership dues for full-time students.

American Consultants League
c/o ETR
245 NE 4th Ave., Suite 102
Delray Beach, FL 33483
americanconsultantsleague.com
Members/Purpose: Full- and part-time consultants in varied fields of expertise.
Training: Offers a home study program.
Journals/Publications: *Consulting Success Library*; directory; consulting tips newsletter
Job Listings: None

American Historical Association
400 A St. SE
Washington, DC 20003
historians.org
Members/Purpose: Professional historians, educators, and others interested in promoting historical studies and collecting and preserving historical manuscripts.
Training: None
Journals/Publications: *Perspectives*; *American Historical Review*; *Directory of Historical Departments and Organizations in the United States and Canada*; other directories and publications
Job Listings: Offers job listings.

American Library Association
50 E. Huron St.
Chicago, IL 60611
ala.org
Members/Purpose: Librarians, libraries, trustees, friends of libraries, and others interested in the responsibilities of libraries in the educational and cultural needs of society.
Journals/Publications: ALA handbook of organization and membership directory; *American Libraries*; *Booklist*; *ALA TechSource*; *Book Links*; *Choice*
Job Listings: Offers placement services; see American Libraries for listings.

American Society for Information Science and Technology
1320 Fenwick Ln., Suite 510
Silver Spring, MD 20910
asis.org
Members/Purpose: Information specialists, scientists, librarians, administrators, social scientists, and others interested in the use, organization, storage, retrieval, evaluation, and dissemination of recorded specialized information.
Training: Conducts continuing education programs and professional development workshops.
Journals/Publications: *Annual Review of Information Science and Technology*; bulletin; *Journal of the American Society for Information Science*; digital library
Job Listings: Maintains placement service.

American Society for Legal History
c/o New York Law School
57 Worth St.
New York, NY 10013
h-net.msu.edu/~/aw/ASLH/aslh.htm
Members/Purpose: Judges; lawyers; law educators; history, political science, and economics professors; historians, students, and others.
Training: None
Journals/Publications: *ASLH Newsletter*; *Law and History Review*; *Studies in Legal History*
Job Listings: None

Association for Canadian Studies
1822 A Sherbrooke W
Montreal, QC H3H 1E4
acs-aec.ca
Members/Purpose: Supports activities in research, teaching, communications, and the training of students in the field of Canadian Studies, especially in interdisciplinary and multidisciplinary perspectives. Works to raise public awareness of Canadian issues, and provides the Canadian Studies community, principally within Canada, with a wide range of activities and programs.
Training: Holds annual conference and other conferences; sponsors travel and research programs.
Journals/Publications: *Canadian Studies*; *CARS*; *Canadian Diversity*
Job Listings: None

Association for Operations Management

5301 Shawnee Rd.

Alexandria, VA 23212

apics.org

Members/Purpose: Organization of professionals in various areas of systems and operations management.

Training: Offers professional development opportunities in operations management.

Journal/Publication: *APICS Magazine*

Job Listings: Offers online career center.

Association of Professional Consultants

P.O. Box 51193

Irvine, CA 92619-1193

consultapc.org

Members/Purpose: Professional consultants.

Training: None

Journals/Publications: Member directory; business directory; speaker directory; newsletters

Job Listings: None

Canadian Historical Association

395 Wellington

Ottawa, ON K1A 0N4

cha-shc.ca

Members/Purpose: Operates as a bilingual organization dedicated to scholarship in all fields of history. Serves professional historians but membership is open to anyone with an interest in history. Represents the interests of historians and the heritage community to government, archives, granting and other agencies; organizes conferences; publishes Canadian historical scholarship; awards a range of prizes to historians who have produced exceptional work.

Training: Annual meeting and other conferences.

Journals/Publications: *Journal of the Canadian Historical Association*; historical booklets; ethnic groups booklets; *Canadian Historical Association Bulletin*

Job Listings: None

Canadian Library Association

328 Frank St.

Ottawa, ON K2P 0X8

cla.ca

Members/Purpose: Functions as a national library association representing approximately 2,500 institutional and personal members. Serves as a monitor and advocate on political and economic issues that affect libraries and library staff; advises members on issues such as copyright, taxation on books, information policy, and censorship.

Training: Sponsors an annual conference and various professional development opportunities.

Journals/Publications: Offers a variety of studies, reports, and other titles including *Training in Caps Analysis—Librarians and Library Technicians*; *8Rs—The Future of Human Resources in Canadian Libraries*; *Achieving Information Literacy: Standards for School Library Programs in Canada*; *Demystifying Copyright: A Researcher's Guide to Copyright in Canadian Libraries and Archives*

Job Listings: Offers a Web-based career section.

Organization of American Historians
112 N. Bryan Ave.
Bloomington, IN 47407
oah.org

Members/Purpose: Professional historians, including college faculty members, secondary school teachers, graduate students, and other individuals in related fields. Promotes historical study and research in the field of American history.

Training: None

Journals/Publications: *Journal of American History*; *OAH Newsletter*; *OAH Magazine of History*

Job Listings: See *OAH Newsletter*.

Society for Nonprofit Organizations
5820 Canton Center Rd., Suite 165
Canton, MI 48187
snpo.org

Members/Purpose: Executive directors, staff, board members, volunteers, and other professionals who serve nonprofit organizations.

Training: Sponsors seminars and workshops on nonprofit management and leadership.

Journals/Publications: *Nonprofit World*; *National Directory of Service/Product Providers*; *Funding Alert*

Job Listings: Offers online job information.

Special Libraries Association
331 S. Patrick St.
Alexandria, VA 22314
sla.org
Members/Purpose: International association of information professionals who work in special libraries serving business, research, government, universities, newspapers, museums, and institutions that use or produce specialized information.
Training: Conducts continuing education courses.
Journals/Publications: *Information Outlook Online*; e-newsletters; chapter and division publications
Job Listings: Offers online career center.

9

Path 4: Business Administration and Management

The fields of management and business administration represent perhaps the broadest spectrum of employment for the history major. They also offer tremendous potential for the best use of all you've learned in earning your degree. The broad scope of business allows for many possible "sites" to use different foci of your skill base. Business administration and management are going to demand many, many of the skills the history major acquires in the course of his or her education. History is the record of time, animated and personalized through humanity's failures and accomplishments. History students learn not only the sweep and panoply of human endeavor, but also to see and anticipate patterns of behavior, ingredients for conflict, signs of progress, and a host of other interpretations as they read and analyze the historical facts.

That ability to read and digest information, to collect information, to make sense of events, to draw conclusions, and to perform analyses based on what you've seen and read is the very quality all competitive enterprises need. The historical facts may be increases in foreign competition, changes in product demand, outdated technology, new domestic competitors, marketing challenges, environmental considerations, regulatory demands, or any of the countless situations in an organization that call out for someone to go out and comprehensively review a situation, analyze the facts, draw some conclusions, and then make some recommendations for change based on that analysis.

So, at this point you may be thinking, "Yes, I can do that. I just hadn't thought about my history degree and skills in that way. But now that I read about it, I see that I do have valuable skills that will work in business administration and management." The important point in understanding all of this is, just as you hadn't seen your skills in this new light, your employer will also need to be educated. Your first big job, even before you're hired, is to educate a potential employer about history majors and what they have to offer, how they can be utilized within an organization, and what kinds of jobs they can be put to work doing for the betterment of the organization.

Let's take another look at those skills a history major brings to the job search.

Reading/Retention

More than many other majors, history involves copious amounts of reading, and many history majors become proficient at reading and digesting large amounts of printed material. In fact, your reading skills may have been one of the reasons you decided to major in history. Business administration and management activities place just as much of a premium on reading, and you may have to do as much reading, if not more, than you did as a student. Business reports, newspapers, magazines (both industrial and commercial), faxes, transcripts, trial records, and computer printouts documenting all facets of business activity all come into an organization every day. The organization itself creates correspondence, memorandums, reports, digests, fact sheets, and thousands of other pieces of reading material.

With all this reading, it's no wonder an organization would value and esteem an individual who can read and retain what he or she has read. Some of this material might be culled and edited for an interoffice communications piece, or it may simply be brought out as an important and related fact of interest at a board meeting. Most important, you will bring the knowledge and information from your reading to bear on all your actions and decisions for the employer. The better informed the decision maker, the better the decision is an axiom highly revered in the business community.

Data Collection

Every business enterprise creates its own history every day. Not every business is equally adept at handling the organization and holdings of the tangible records of that history, whether they are computer printouts or sample packaging materials. Very often, the organization is not aware of the importance of this material to their future. Though they frequently may bemoan the loss of some important document or piece of information, they do not and cannot relate that to their current poor practices for data collection and maintenance.

Step right in, history major, and take charge. You'll have an innate sense of what an organization needs to store, what it needs to keep at the ready in terms of data. If data collection is not providing the information a firm needs to do the job, you'll have recommendations on redesigning the data collection documents. In reading and studying your history, you've continually had to separate the relevant from the irrelevant as you follow a historical fact or event over time. The need is no different in an organization except that the process can always be improved. You can make a real difference here!

Research

This category speaks for itself and is probably one that you would immediately feel comfortable talking about with a prospective employer. Research is the preeminent skill of the student of history and it has equal value in all other areas of human endeavor. Because you've used your research talents consistently over the course of your college career, you've amassed an unusual amount of research techniques, some of which may be unconscious. Along the way, you may have enjoyed some specific library technique classes or become proficient in the use of searchable databases on the computer. Many libraries now offer direct CD-ROM access to many informational databases including full-text downloadable resources. A professor who assigned a research paper may have had one of the library staff brief your class on library research procedures.

In addition to the training, you've had on-the-job experience with numerous papers, reports, and formal research assignments. The content may have been history, but the techniques, the skills, the patience, and perseverance—even the ability to seek professional research assistance—are all common experiences and will be directly applicable to the world of work, whether the topic is the number of men ages fifty and above who vote for female candidates or the relative sugar content in the various fruit drinks available in grocery stores. Notice these two ads:

Research Associate. National think tank located in Washington, DC. Handle research on selected public policy issues including abortion, stem cell research, and civil liberties. Requires minimum of B.A. Send writing samples to . . .

News Production Assistant (Local Television News Station). Research, write, check facts, maintain research library, write/research/edit Web copy, assist with studio production, some driving. Résumé, letter, and writing samples to . . .

Analysis

Facts are just facts until they are digested and analyzed. In any commercial enterprise, there is an ongoing and insistent need for talented people who can look at data and understand what this information represents to the organization. Look at this next ad:

Writer/Researcher. Prepare policy reports and analyses on civil rights issues. Requires excellent writing skills, quantitative skills, know history of civil rights movement and current public policy. B.A. in liberal arts. Résumé and letter to (national civil rights organization) . . .

Critical Thinking

Just as so often happened in your study of history, you will begin to notice, in your review and analysis of any organization's efforts, certain trends and patterns of thinking. Some will be ingredients for success and others will be opportunities to alert the organization to patterns of thinking, behavior, or goal setting that may be unproductive. Perhaps you have noticed that soon after instituting a new annual sale policy, your employer (a manufacturer of golf clubs and golf equipment) began to experience severe drops in customer purchases in the months prior to the annual sale. Your analysis clearly demonstrates that the volume increase generated by the sale is only marginally better than normal annual purchases unstimulated by annual price reduction. You also have found on some customer comment cards a disturbing related fact that some customers may associate sale merchandise with less than top quality. Your presentation to management will challenge the organization with important ideas and considerations.

Writing/Communication

Just as history changes, so, too, does the way in which history is communicated. We are grateful for the great work of historians past such as Gibbon, Chabod, and Toynbee. Today, our new television historians communicate by actively demonstrating and walking us through the Parthenon before Europeans explored North America. We know and appreciate that history needs to be communicated in writing, through the spoken word, and with the help of our ever-increasing armory of visual technology. Your own experience as a student has given you a sense for those writings, texts, films, and other material that made the subject vivid and the issues easily understood. Your task in business will be to use the means at hand to communicate your findings. It may be anything from a simple memo to an interactive television seminar beamed across the country or the world. Notice the importance placed on communication in this ad:

Public Outreach Coordinator. Conduct community outreach to high school students, college students, church youth groups, residents of halfway houses, parents, youth workers, and other groups. Design and deliver seminars and workshops on avoiding unsafe sexual practices. Provide information to youth and families on preventing pregnancies and diseases. Make referrals to appropriate agencies. Strong presentation skills required. Qualifications: related work experience or college education; commitment to mission of organization; persistence; computer literacy; reliable transportation. Salary package includes excellent benefits. Send résumé and cover letter to (Planned Parenthood affiliate) . . .

Don't let your unfamiliarity with technology or the teaching role throw you. Those techniques can be learned on the job. It is most important to communicate to your employer your ability to describe, explain, illustrate, and demonstrate what you have to say. A simple portfolio of some of your representative work would be a helpful and practical demonstration of this.

Prescriptions for Change

Some very large firms may have company historians, but there aren't very many. In fact, that job is more likely to be given to a very senior employee who may have no formal history training but has lived the history of the organization. The variety of skills you are offering to an organization argue for a more active, involved role in company planning and decision making.

One of the results of data analysis and the recognition of trends and recurring issues is the possibility of understanding the ingredients for success as well as avoiding the path to disaster. Your history training has taught you to be aware of events and their short- and long-term effects on ultimate causes. It's no different in the organization. When you do discover a pattern, it will be a natural thing to propose some solutions to apply to the situation.

Perhaps you are looking at customer traffic in a chain of coffee shops owned by your organization. In analyzing cash register printouts and management reports, you notice a consistent drop in business in midafternoon and again after the dinner hour and long before closing. You have high overhead and a full staff you cannot afford to have idle. You propose offering an afternoon "coffee hour" with reduced pricing to attract patrons out shopping or businesspeople needing a place to stop and talk and enjoy light refreshment. For the evening lull, you propose entertainment such as poetry readings. None of these ideas makes heavy demands on costs since the coffee shop is already operating during those hours and the additional items are easily produced. Your research and analysis could lead to a new business strategy, increased customer traffic, improved profitability, and a new dimension of services and products for your company. History in the making.

Definition of the Career Path

We've made the case for history majors in business administration and management. They're needed, they have important skills, and there are jobs they can do. Now, you very logically ask yourself, "How do I get started finding those jobs? Where will my career start and how will it progress? What employers should I begin calling on in my job search and what will they call the jobs I qualify to do?" These are all excellent and legitimate questions. Let's take a look at some actual job listings as we begin our discussion of the career path for history majors in business administration and management positions:

Sales Coordinator. Fast-growing private label importer/mfr located in picturesque waterfront town seeks energetic, detail-oriented professional. Primary respon. will include: product sourcing, price negotiations, placing and tracking orders, sales and maintenance of production status. Int'l and domestic travel required. Should have degree or 3–4 yrs related work experience. Send résumé and salary requirements to . . .

This position is an excellent example of the kind of entry-level position for which a history major should apply because it uses so many skills you have acquired in your studies. Let's look more closely at the position.

Here's a firm that both manufactures and imports products to be purchased and relabeled by other firms. The private label sector of the economy is a huge industry, as many excellent products and manufacturers simply do not have the name recognition nor the marketing expertise to create a strong brand name image for their organization. They find it easier to either sell their products to another organization to be relabeled or manufacture products to a large organization's specifications. Most of these firms lie outside the United States where hourly wages are lower and cost of goods is proportionately cheaper, allowing for significant markups of products as they pass through the chain of distribution to the consumer.

This position requires an energetic individual. This is a personal quality that you will have assessed through your completion of the self-evaluation that opens this book. It is probably part of the job announcement because the organization is fast-paced, management may be young and very active, or there may be fewer staff filling many different roles. Pay attention to demands such as this and be honest in your response. If you're not particularly energetic and choose to misrepresent your energy level to acquire the position, soon enough both your real temperament and that of the organization will become apparent, and that will be a stressful situation for both parties.

The next demand is for "detail orientation." Certainly, a student of history is not only detail-oriented but aware of the crucial importance of details in decision making and in planning and strategy. If your contracting firm wants a product made out of one-hundred percent recycled paper, you'll know that doesn't mean seventy-five or eighty percent, and before you make some independent decision you would go back to your contracting buyer and determine how critical that product specification is.

The responsibilities of this job for sourcing products, negotiating prices, tracking orders, and monitoring the status of production runs are a wonderful demonstration of the practical applications of the skills we outlined in the introduction. Reading and retention, data collection, research, analysis, and critical thinking would all be skills needed every day in this exciting position.

The position also suggests travel experience, international and domestic, would be helpful. This is another personal qualification. Perhaps you have little travel experience at this point in your life. The employer for this job might be less concerned about that qualification if, during the interview, you displayed a high level of general information about world events, world politics, foreign exchange rates, and the gold standard. The demand for travel may be simply the employer's belief that the individual who has traveled is going to be more aware and more culturally sensitive when conducting business over the telephone, in person, and by letter to business contacts of other cultures.

Let's look at some other actual position descriptions and see what we can learn about the jobs and your qualifications for them:

Health Management Associate. (Major insurance company) will train in all aspects of health management including sales and marketing, operations, and tech analysis. Requires B.A./B.S., math or quantitative skills, and excellent oral and written communication skills. Résumé, letter, transcripts, and salary requirements to ...

Researcher/Writer. Growing mgt consult firm. Requires B.A., excellent analytical, writing, and communication skills, and creativity. Résumé and letter to ...

Both these positions share a common interest in a candidate that has both strong communications skills *and* an analytical orientation. Each position seems to suggest significant research, data collection, and analysis demands. One explicitly refers to the personal qualification of creativity, while the other (management trainee), because of its association with sales and marketing, may equally value that attribute in a candidate. Both look like excellent entry-level positions for a student of history who wants to use his or her academic preparation in the areas of business administration and management.

Working Conditions

As you read these job announcements and contemplate a business career, you may feel both excitement and hesitation. Excitement at the idea that, yes, your skills are valuable and many employers seem to be asking for candidates with talents and attributes similar to those you have developed and perfected in your studies as a history major.

At the same time, you may only recently have begun to think of employment in a concrete way and somehow never imagined yourself in a corporation or wearing a business suit and carrying a briefcase. You may sense that businesses and even larger, more organized nonprofit organizations have more rules about conduct, appearance, manners, and hierarchy than you have been used to or would enjoy. After all, part of your decision to major in history might have been a disdain for some of the same work orientation or profit motive that prompted your classmates to major in business or computer science. Now here you are also considering the world of business administration and management and justifiably wondering, will you fit in?

Rest assured that the world of work is as diverse as the population in general and it is populated with peoples of differing interests, political persuasions, lifestyles, values, and talents. There is certainly room for you, too. Your skills are valued and needed, and most organizations realize that, along with your talent and education, you come with a particular philosophy and even, perhaps, a different lifestyle.

But we'd like to suggest that some changes may have to be made. After all, a corporation is a public entity and its employees represent the organization. How they look, act, and communicate while they represent the organization affect the business and, ultimately, their livelihood. Publicly traded companies with shareholders may feel this responsibility to a greater degree than the private company or family-held business. Nevertheless, a business's success rises and falls on its ability to maintain good relations with its publics.

Businesses today have become much more sophisticated about their staffs and their needs. Some offer flexible time scheduling with varying arrival and departure times for different workers. Some will allow two employees to "share" a job, each splitting it in half. This kind of benefit has been helpful for parents who are interested in staying home with young children. Some larger organizations offer on-site child or elder care, demonstrating a real recognition of home and scheduling problems. An increasing number of firms are offering benefits to same-sex couples and recognizing same-sex couples in social functions and invitations to those functions. Drug, alcohol, and emotional issues are more out in the open, and firms often offer counseling and referral services for these problems, and do so discreetly and without the stigma these problems earned employees in corporations of the past.

Many firms now offer memberships in health and fitness clubs or actually have those kinds of clubs on site as part of their benefits program. Of course, this emphasis on exercise and diet has beneficial effects on productivity and reduced absenteeism but, even more than that, it builds self-esteem as participants become prouder of how they look and feel and bring that pride into their work. It increases camaraderie and cuts across all hierarchical lines as different kinds of workers meet in the gym and weight rooms.

It might be easy to believe that because an organization is not for profit and may be deeply involved in doing good in the world, many of the conditions so firmly set in a corporation would not be found in the not for profit. While certainly many nonprofit organizations have very relaxed norms for all their activities, a great many others feel that to gain the private and public dollars needed and to inspire public trust, they need to present the same picture of organization, sophistication, and determination as a corporation.

Competitiveness is another reasonable concern. Are corporate climates all that competitive, or is that the stuff of myth making? Certainly as a history major you competed for grades, and though you were largely competing with yourself and past performance, you were in a sense competing with a class standard set by all members. Business is no different. While most competitive initiative is *outwardly* directed, toward other firms, there are certainly performance norms established over time by the general level of expertise in the firm. Because in large part you are hired with these norms in mind, and your résumé and experience are evaluated on criteria already established for success in the organization, you will do fine. It is important that you stay "tuned in" as an employee to performance standards and do your best to maintain your contribution.

You will participate in periodic evaluations with your direct supervisor to review your accomplishments and set appropriate goals for yourself for the next evaluation period. These evaluations will be the proper setting to discuss your understanding and appreciation of your job, your desire for additional training, or ideas for job modification.

Training and Qualifications

Our review of some sample advertisements has made it clear that, along with your history education, computer familiarity, quantitative skills, and general business knowledge would all be helpful. If your curriculum allows for it, see about adding a general business course or selected introductory courses in accounting, management, economics, and operations. Don't neglect your quantitative education, either. Though your love of history may be directly in inverse proportion to your dislike of math, your analytical skills will often be applied to data involving numbers, and you'll approach this part of your job with more comfort if you have kept your skills well honed. The following recent advertisement calls for several of these skills:

Office Coordinator. Full-time position for a professional, self-motivated individual who is able to work independently. Responsibilities will focus on the coordination of physician credentialing and the compilation and organization of statistical information related to physician activities. Must be detail-oriented to ensure compliance with all medical staff bylaws and pertinent standards. Strong interpersonal skills needed to interface with all levels of the organization. Proficiency required in Word with previous database experience. B.A./B.S. and previous experience in medical/hospital desired. Please forward résumé and salary requirements to (regional health clinic) . . .

This general business education will help you to appreciate your employer's business situation, improve your communication at interviews, and speed your research activities when investigating certain industries or specific companies. Some schools offer an introduction to nonprofit organizations, which would be of help to anyone interested in that employment sector.

Any kind of business internship would also assure an employer of your interest in applying your history skills in the public arena. You might look at internships in research, office administration, development, or rotating assignments where you have the opportunity to spend some time in all the departments of an organization. You'll come away from such an experience with a strong sense of what you could do for a firm and how an organization functions.

Earnings

Because of the breadth of this employment category, starting salaries are a function of both the general salaries in the industry you are looking at (salaries in industry will be higher than in consumer service firms) and your particular set of skills. The more specific skills (computer, math, research, and so forth) you bring in addition to your degree, the higher your initial salary range. Generally, entry-level salaries in the high twenties or thirties, and in some cases higher, can be expected.

Career Outlook

The kinds of positions we have been discussing are sometimes referred to as "generalist" positions because they are not technical and the educational background required is rather loose in terms of demand. Additionally, with these generalist positions there are no firmly established criteria for entry-level positions. Much depends on the employer being approached and the particular combination of skills, talent, and personality of the applicant and how that combination fits. The hiring outlook has much to do with the general trend of the economy and the size and location of the hiring organization. These types of positions often follow economic trends. If, for example, an industry and the employers within that sector are not doing well, what monies those employers have to spend on hiring new employees will probably first go toward technical expertise to improve efficiency and product quality and then to financial management staff to ensure fiscal control and solvency. The entry-level general administrator with "soft" or untried skills is not an attractive commodity at such times.

When personnel staffing monies are somewhat more available, it is easier to find and fill these positions. A corollary of this information is that these positions are also more likely to be early casualties in a downturn in the economy through layoffs, reductions in force, enforced leaves of absence, or dismissals for financial exigencies. To prevent this situation, you are encouraged to use your employed time to acquire more specific skills that would significantly alter your résumé. A good example of this would be how you could self-manage for growth in an entry-level position as a human resource associate for a large nonprofit organization. Perhaps you have been hired as an assistant benefits administrator, briefing new employees on benefit program choices and assisting in managing the smooth flow of paperwork and forms surrounding the filing and paying of claims. You could do this job in an exemplary manner for three years and yet still only be qualified for an identical job somewhere else.

Or you could request cross-training in Occupational Safety and Health Administration (OSHA) guidelines for workers, participate in professional development programs to learn more about pay classification guidelines, volunteer to work on the team producing a new benefits brochure or Web page and pick up copywriting and graphics experience, and enroll and participate in every training opportunity provided. Ask your boss if you can sit in on contract negotiations when benefit packages are up for renewal. Soon you will discover you have built a substantial body of expertise in your field.

No longer are you a generalist with only your degree in history to recommend you, but you are now qualified as a payroll specialist, a benefits officer, an employee trainer, or even director of human resources for a smaller organization.

Strategies for Finding the Jobs

There are many ways to prepare for the job search in business administration and management, but we have highlighted five efforts that we believe should be included in the history major's strategy. First, it is important that you realize and communicate the skill base that your study of history has brought you. Then it will be important to identify which employers need and value your skills. Use the research skills you've developed, and the tips and techniques presented in this book, to find out as much as you can about industry trends and specific employers. Then you must highlight how you can help these organizations and, finally, be proactive as well as reactive in your search.

Realize and Communicate the Skill Base That Your Study of History Has Brought You

In the introduction to the career path, we described a series of skills that the history major develops and enhances in gaining his or her degree. You are able to read volumes of information and retain it, research and collect relevant data, then analyze it and create information. You are able to identify themes, trends, and patterns, write and speak about what you've observed, and make recommendations for change. All of these are valued in business, industry, and commerce, and it is your job to highlight these skills for potential employers. You don't want them guessing about your potential value to the organization, so make it very clear. Be sure to review the chapter on résumés and cover letters, and the one on interviewing, for specific techniques on writing and communicating these important skills.

Learn Which Types of Employers Need and Value These Skills

Your talents, skills, and abilities are valued by every type of employer we can think of, so you will have to use some other criteria to narrow down the types of jobs you will apply for. Think about hobbies and interests you may have; oftentimes there are ways to combine your interests and the work you do. If you're a hand weaver, you might consider examining administrative positions available with professional associations serving the textile industry; if you have played baseball since you were a child, you might consider sales positions with sports equipment manufacturers. Work with a career counselor to explore ways to tie your interests to the world of work. You'll probably be surprised at the connections you'll find.

Find Out About Industry Trends and Specific Employers

Once you determine a focus for beginning a job search, you'll want to educate yourself about the industry in general and specific employers in particular. Consult resources such as Hoovers.com, and then use websites and e-mail to contact appropriate industry associations for more detailed materials. You'll also want to use references like jigsaw.com, *Hoover's Handbook of American Business,* or *Ward's Business Directory of Private and Public Companies in Canada* to find out about individual employers. Many excellent resources are available, so be sure to consult with your career counselor or the librarian you're working with. This background information will help you formulate a résumé and speak in an informed way as you begin interviewing.

Highlight How You Can Help These Organizations

Previously we described a set of skills that your history degree helped you build. Each employment setting will place a different value on each skill, viewing some skills as more important than others. It's your job to highlight these skills in a meaningful way for each employer. You may have to revamp your résumé for different types of jobs or different industries. Remember, you must identify the relevant pieces of your history that show an employer you are capable of and qualified to do the work they need done.

Be Proactive as Well as Reactive

Your job search must have two thrusts. First, reacting to actual job listings, and, second, networking with potential employers to find out about hidden jobs.

Be Reactive. Everyone can stay up to date on newspaper job listings via the Internet by using search engines such as Google or LookSmart.com. They will direct you to classified listings all over the United States (and Canada, if you use "Canada" or Canadian" as one of your search terms). Most career offices on college campuses can connect you on the Internet to their own free electronic job posting services as well as many free and some fee-based job posting services. But did you also know that most professional associations or organizations publish newsletters, available only to members, that contain job listings? A college or university library will house some of these publications, your career office may have others, and some faculty will also subscribe. Be sure to check with people in your network to determine the range of job listings available to you.

Don't Forget to Be Proactive. Use your college or university alumni career network to talk with professionals who are working in the type of job you hope to get or who are working in an industry that interests you. Be sure to contact relevant professional associations for information on job-related services that you might want to take advantage of. Just a few of these associations are listed at the end of this path. Your career counselor may have additional suggestions based on your interests. Conducting a job search can take a lot of time, so carefully choose who you will spend your time networking with.

Possible Employers

You'll be pleasantly surprised at the range of firms that hire history degree holders. Consider the following types of companies:

Advertising departments and agencies
Airlines, railroads, and cruise lines
Banks, savings and loans, credit unions
Environmentally related firms
Federal government
Hospitals and other health-care companies
Hotels, motels, and hospitality industry employers
Magazines, newspapers, radio stations, cable networks, television stations
Manufacturing firms
Nonprofit organizations
Professional associations
Public relations departments and firms
Sports-related organizations

Decide where you'd like to begin your search and use the resources listed to help you locate that particular type of employer.

Advertising Departments and Agencies

Among the most interesting employment opportunities are those offered in the world of advertising. Every effective advertising campaign relies on the work of market researchers to answer questions such as, Should a product be made? Who will buy it? Where should it be sold? How much should be charged? Entry-level market researchers usually work on questionnaire development, coding, and data entry. They research data found in libraries and assist in project report writing.

Where You Might Fit In. If in obtaining your degree you found enjoyment in doing research, crunching numbers, reporting results, or keeping track of details, market research may be one type of advertising job you'd like to find out more about. Two major suppliers of research include Simmons Market Research Bureau (smrb.com) and Mediamark Research Inc. (mediamark.com). Both of these firms supply secondary data on product usage and consumption. Nielson/NetRatings (netratings.com) and Arbitron (dealerdata.arbitron.com) also provide statistics used by advertising agencies. Market researchers provide the ammunition that other advertising professionals need to promote customers' products or services.

Help in Locating These Employers. If you would like to identify the larger agencies that would typically hire this type of worker, you can use several resources. McGraw-Hill's *Careers in Advertising*, *Adweek*, and adagency jobs.net, among others, will provide potentially helpful information on employers you could consider approaching.

Airlines, Railroads, and Cruise Lines

Transportation, travel, and tourism all hold many possibilities for the person who majored in history. In fact, you may have even specialized in transportation history or the history of a sport such as skiing. You can bring your deep understanding or specialized knowledge to your work in these industries.

Where You Might Fit In. No matter what skills you possess, the tourism, travel, and transportation industries need them. If you have effective interpersonal communication skills, you may be interested in a customer service position as a travel agent, purser, or customer service representative. If you prefer to hold a less public job, positions in functional areas such as computer services or research and marketing might interest you.

Help in Locating These Employers. Quite a number of helpful resources can be found in career and public libraries. These include *Becoming a Tour Guide, Global Travel and Tourism Career Opportunities, Jobs in the Sun, Cruise Operations Management, Opportunities in Hotel & Motel Management Careers, How to Start a Tour Guiding Business,* and *Timeshare Resort Operations.* Check each of these and read chapters or sections that will inform your job search.

Banks, Savings and Loans, and Credit Unions

One of the most rapidly changing areas of the financial services industry is that of banks and other savings institutions. The financial industry includes commercial banks, thrifts, mutual savings banks, savings and loan associations, and credit unions. Services usually include deposit and loan services, general customer service, business services, municipal services, trust services, and international banking services.

Where You Might Fit In. When you think of banking, do you also think of corporate communications, planning, legal departments, marketing, operations, personnel, public relations, purchasing, or training? Large financial institutions include these departments as well. And your liberal arts degree in history will be valued in many of the positions available in any of these departments.

Help in Locating These Employers. Several types of resources are available if you would like to learn more about this industry. Be sure to check *Hoover's Hand-*

book of American Business, the yellow pages for geographic areas in which you're interested, and Web pages of U.S. and Canadian financial institutions.

Environmentally Related Firms

The environment is hot, at least from a career viewpoint. History majors will find themselves among those who can find challenging jobs in this area.

There are firms that assess the environmental impact of proposed building projects, firms that sell pollution-control equipment, respond to and clean up hazardous waste spills, and are responsible for solid-waste disposal. The state of the environment is an issue that no one can ignore, and job opportunities are increasing with growing awareness of this problem.

Where You Might Fit In. Some of these organizations need your researching and writing skills to help prepare proposals that might bring in new business. If you are comfortable making presentations to groups, you could become part of a sales team that sells environmentally related products or services. You might have an interest in human resources and can work for the organization in helping it acquire the personnel it needs to carry out specific and technical duties.

Help in Locating These Employers. One way to begin identifying potential employers, like an international pollution control monitoring manufacturer, is to find the Standard Industrial Code (SIC) for this type of company. Business.com (business.com) is one source that lists these codes. There are many different types of pollution-control monitoring manufacturers, and some of the SIC codes that are used include 3564, 3589, 8417, 8418, and 8421. The codes can then be used in identifying companies that might be potential employers in this area. Also, add to your growing list of potential employers by checking the yellow pages (both your local and Internet variety), consulting job sites such as Monster.com and Best Jobs Canada (bestjobsca.com), and using a Web search engine to seek out companies under headings such as "Environmental," "Conservation," or "Ecological Services."

Federal Government

The U.S. and Canadian governments are some of the largest employers in the world. They employ workers in hundreds of governmental departments, agencies, commissions, bureaus, and boards.

Where You Might Fit In. Government agencies that may be specifically interested in hiring history majors include the U.S. Department of Justice (usdoj.gov/dea), National Endowment for the Humanities (neh.gov), National Park Service (nps.gov), Smithsonian Institution (si.edu), U.S. Customs and Border Protection (customs.treasury.gov), U.S. Information Agency (usinfo.state.gov), National Research Council Canada (nrc-cnrc.gc.ca), Natural Resources Canada (nrcan-rncan.gc.ca), and the Public Service Commission of Canada (psc-cfp.gc.ca). In fact, a wide range of agencies regularly hire college graduates with degrees in any of the liberal arts, including history, for positions in environmental protection, public health, public affairs, technical information services, bond sales promotion, building management, financial administration, housing management, employee development, and examining workers compensation claims. This list certainly is not comprehensive; your exploration of federal job opportunities will reveal many more job titles and functions.

Help in Locating These Employers. Because federal employment is a complicated process, given the number of possible employment sites and job titles, we encourage you to take the time to really explore all the possibilities in federal employment. The premier website for federal job postings is usajobs.opm.gov, but also consult other online job sites such as Best Jobs Canada (bestjobsca.com) along with books such as McGraw-Hill's *Opportunities in Government Careers.*

Hospitals and Other Health-Care Companies

Perhaps no area of the economy offers more future career potential than the health-care industry. While many jobs are restricted to highly trained specialists, there is also room for generalists.

Many large hospitals are cities unto themselves, and like health-care companies employ workers from janitors to doctors, billing clerks to nurses, social science researchers to employee assistance coordinators. In many places, the graduate of history can find "a good fit."

Where You Might Fit In. We recently saw an advertisement for a sales staff coordinator that required someone who can work independently compiling and organizing statistical information related to activities of a large national sales force. The position required computer proficiency and preferred experience in a business setting, but did not require it, and also asked for a bachelor's degree. Any history major with these credentials would be qualified to apply.

Help in Locating These Employers. Helpful resources include *Careers in Health Care, Opportunities in Holistic Health Care Careers, Top 100 Health-Care Careers,* and *Health Care Job Explosion: High Growth Health Care Careers.*

Also, a website that can help you locate any hospital or medical facility in the country may be accessed at hospitaldirectories.com.

Hotels, Motels, and Hospitality Industry Employers

The lodging industry is well known for moving dedicated and conscientious entry-level workers into higher-level managerial positions. It is also known for its excellent training programs, which provide the skills necessary to make these promotions. Large resorts and hotels have correspondingly large operations, which include housekeeping, food service, convention facilities, fitness centers, laundry, purchasing, human resources, and marketing departments.

Where You Might Fit In. These larger facilities often hire convention and meeting planners. Planners are in charge of putting together a variety of events that help increase facility use. Whether it's planning a conference for archaeologists, an awards dinner that includes three hundred guests, or a meeting of scientists and journalists discussing global warming, all have their special space utilization needs, and attention to detail is critical.

Help in Locating These Employers. Books that can provide useful information on working in the hospitality industry and are worth reviewing are *Opportunities in Hotel & Motel Careers, Opportunities in Restaurant Careers, Introduction to Management in the Hospitality Industry, Student Workbook,* and *Hotel/Restaurant Career Starter.*

Magazines, Newspapers, Radio Stations, Cable Networks, Television Stations

If you examine the sheer volume of activity in this sector of the economy, you'll realize you have many employment possibilities to consider. There are thousands of general circulation magazines, daily newspapers, radio stations, television stations, cable television, and satellite systems operating in the United States and Canada, not to mention the many websites that offer news or entertainment. They employ writers, editors, promotion specialists, production managers, public relations specialists, researchers, librarians, and reporters. Many, many entry-level positions are filled by liberal arts majors, including history majors.

Where You Might Fit In. Commercial and public television stations are required by the Federal Communications Commission (FCC) to provide public service announcements on the air, and community affairs directors coordinate these efforts at larger stations. These directors play a role in planning, writing, producing, hosting, narrating, moderating, and editing announcements, programs, and documentaries. The history major who writes well, has strong organizational and communications skills, and has an interest in working in television would be an excellent candidate for entry-level positions in this type of division.

Help in Locating These Employers. There certainly is no lack of relevant reference materials when it comes to careers in publishing, radio and TV, and communications. For direction in locating potential employers, look at *Careers in Communications, Publishers Directory, Career Opportunities in Television and Cable, Gale Directory of Publications and Broadcast Media, Starting Your Career in Broadcasting,* and *Opportunities in Broadcasting Careers.*

Manufacturing Firms

The most frequently overlooked area of employment for many liberal arts degree majors is the area of manufacturing. Pharmaceuticals, machine-tooled parts, automobiles, plastics and polymers, and countless subcontracted component parts are bought and sold around the world to specification. Whether in South America, the Pacific Rim, or Eastern Europe, or at an import-export desk here at home, history majors will find they do not want to ignore manufacturing.

Where You Might Fit In. In reality, manufacturing mimics every other segment of the economy. It advertises, transports, finances, restructures, repositions itself, and produces all the associated trappings of any business. What's more, it is populated and managed by skilled, educated people from a multiplicity of backgrounds, including history. Nearly all of the job titles described in other sections of this book can be found in the manufacturing sector, including communications specialist, transport scheduler, controller, planner, public relations specialist, media planner, trainer, or benefits administrator, just to name a few.

Help in Locating These Employers. Manufacturing firms are listed in *American Manufacturers Directory, Ward's Business Directory of U.S. Private and Public Companies, Business Rankings Annual, Almanac of American Employers,* and *Hoover's Handbook of American Business.* Manufacturers may be listed by industry or by standard industrial code; if you are not familiar with these breakdowns, don't hesitate to ask the resource person on duty in your career office or library to help you with locating companies.

Nonprofit Organizations

Want to lend a helping hand? The nonprofit sector includes organizations involved in issues ranging from animal rights to homelessness, hunger to peace and disarmament, and people with disabilities to women's issues. The history major could find a home in many of these organizations, but each would ask that you have a strong belief in their mission and be able to actively help them achieve their goals.

Where You Might Fit In. Nonprofits are creating organizational structures nearly identical to those of the for-profits, so you will find positions available in the same functional areas. Look for positions in human resources, home-office management, field staff direction, finance, accounting, communications, publications, public relations, marketing, membership services, information systems, development, and program management.

Help in Locating These Employers. If you would like to get a sense of the range of opportunities available, be sure to review *The Harvard Business School Guide to Careers in the Nonprofit Sector* or *Careers in Nonprofits and Government Agencies.* Or try contacting the Society for Nonprofit Organizations, located in Canton, Michigan (http://danenet.wicip.org/snpo). In addition, *Community Jobs* (communityjobs.org) is a website that includes actual job listings.

Professional Associations

Like the nonprofit organizations described, professional associations of all types also hire large numbers of people, including liberal arts majors. We frequently urge readers to use professional associations in their job search. They provide information on the professions, training and development, opportunities to meet colleagues, and a never-ending flow of excellent, pertinent literature. However, they are also employers and because of that, we list them in this section as well. While the individual staffs may be small, the number of organizations is huge and together that creates opportunities enough that the history major cannot and should not overlook the serious consideration of the professional association for employment.

With your degree, the association may be academic, commercial, historical, educational, or even partisan. Whatever the specific purpose of the group, your vested interest by virtue of your degree will guarantee that your résumé gets a careful reading. Consider the professional association carefully.

Where You Might Fit In. These organizations make a range of printed materials (booklets, information sheets, magazines, and newspapers) that promote their cause or educate their members. If you have researching, writing, and editing skills, they will be valued. Conference planning and coordination is another area of responsibility in a nonprofit organization. Membership services require excellent communications abilities and may be of interest to you.

Help in Locating These Employers. Two publications that identify these associations are the *Encyclopedia of Associations* and *National Trade and Professional Associations of the United States*. Both of these have several indexes to help you locate associations by geographic region, name, or focus.

Public Relations Departments and Firms

The importance of public relations seems to have grown in recent years. PR professionals play a key role in making organizations successful.

Every client, every challenge presented to a public relations department or firm requires drawing deeply on the talents, resources, and expertise of the professional staff to make the best presentation of the client or product. Imagine the difficulties of representing the fur industry, cigarette manufacturers, or any other controversial product, service, or individual. Public relations work requires being constantly aware of and sensitive to how images and words will be interpreted or understood by the public. The history major has studied the impact of past events on current life and gained a perspective valued in public relations.

Where You Might Fit In. Many of your talents will come into play as a public relations assistant in the acquisition and presentation of data and information to support company positions or strategies being communicated to outside constituencies. Look for organizations with high public visibility, including national chains in the hotel, restaurant, and hospitality industry; major manufacturers of consumer goods, including products subject to litigation (automobiles and children's toys); and, of course, advertising agencies and public relations firms.

Help in Locating These Employers. If you're ready to use your skills in a public relations setting, be sure to review *O'Dwyer's Directory of Public Relations Firms* or the *Vault Guide to the Top Advertising and Public Relations Employers*, or see the "Public Relations Specialists" section in the *Professional Careers Sourcebook*.

Sports-Related Organizations

As just one example, say you have many interests and avocations other than just your college major. You may have been a history major in college but also have a lifelong interest in sports, especially skiing. Your degree and skiing awareness combined make you a promising candidate for many different kinds of positions in this arena.

Where You Might Fit In. You might look for sales positions with manufacturers of ski goggles, gloves, or other products that would use your organizational and communication skills. Or you may be interested in working on the staff of one of the many associations serving skiers, such as U.S. Deaf Ski and Snowboarding Association, Canadian Ski Council, International Free Skiers Association, or National Ski Areas Association researching and analyzing industry data.

Help in Locating These Employers. *Sports Market Place Directory*, an excellent resource, will help you identify thousands of organizations. Included are trade and professional associations, multisport publications, TV and radio broadcasters and programmers, corporate sports sponsors, athletic management services, market data services, trade shows, and suppliers and sales agents. Each entry contains contact information, such as address and telephone number, and also contains background information. Also review *Opportunities in Recreation and Leisure Careers*, *Opportunities in Sports and Fitness Careers*, or *Careers for Sports Nuts & Other Athletic Types* for additional information on the range of opportunities available to you.

Possible Job Titles

Given the range of employers, we'll provide just a few of the many job titles you will find as you do your job search exploration. Watch for these, and add to the list as you study the want ads and online job sites, review resources we've listed, and network with alumni of your institution and other professionals.

    Account representative
    Collaborative projects program officer
    Communications assistant
    Customer service manager
    Financial assistant
    Human resources officer
    Import/export coordinator/expediter
    Income generation specialist
    Loan officer
    Management consultant
    Management trainee
    Manufacturer's representative

Market analyst
Marketing manager
Personnel officer
Pharmaceutical representative
Production assistant
Program director
Program manager
Public relations officer
Research assistant
Salesperson
Tour director
Training and development specialist

Professional Associations

A wide range of employers has been described, and a correspondingly wide range of professional associations is shown below. Examine the list to see which groups you might contact to get additional information about career choices, job opportunities, or professional development assistance. Be sure to use the *Encyclopedia of Associations* or Web searches for the names of other organizations to contact.

American Association of Advertising Agencies
405 Lexington Ave., 18th Floor
New York, NY 10174
aaaa.org
Members/Purpose: To foster, strengthen, and improve the advertising agency business; to advance the cause of advertising as a whole; to aid its member agencies to operate more efficiently and profitably.
Training: None
Journals/Publications: Member bulletins; booklets; Webcasts; podcasts
Job Listings: None

American Bankers Association
1120 Connecticut Ave. NW
Washington, DC 20036
aba.com
Members/Purpose: Commercial banks and trust companies; combined assets of members represent approximately 95 percent of U.S. banking

industry; seeks to enhance the role of commercial banks as preeminent providers of financial services through a variety of efforts.

Training: Offers educational and training programs.

Journals/Publications: *ABA Bankers Weekly*; *ABA Banking Journal*; e-mail bulletins; many other publications and Web resources

Job Listings: None

American Hospital Association
1 N. Franklin
Chicago, IL 60606
aha.org

Members/Purpose: Individuals and health-care institutions including hospitals, health-care systems, and pre- and post-acute health-care delivery organizations.

Training: Conducts educational programs.

Journals/Publications: *AHA News*; *Hospitals and Health Networks*; *Health Facilities Management*

Job Listings: Provides weekly job listing for members.

Hospitality Sales and Marketing Association International
8201 Greensboro Dr.
McLean, VA 22102
hsmai.org

Members/Purpose: Sales executives, managers, owners, and other hospitality industry executives; people from allied fields; other individuals and firms.

Training: Conducts seminars, clinics, and workshops.

Journals/Publications: *Marketing Review*; *HSMAI Update*; chapter newsletters; directory

Job Listings: None

Magazine Publishers of America
810 Seventh Ave.
New York, NY 10019
magazine.org

Members/Purpose: Publishers of more than 1,400 consumer and other magazines.

Training: Sponsors seminars.

Journals/Publications: *Magazine Newsletters* and surveys

Job Listings: None

National Association of Broadcasters
1771 N St. NW
Washington, DC 20036
nab.org
Members/Purpose: Representatives of radio and TV stations and TV networks.
Training: None
Journals/Publications: Conference proceedings; issue papers
Job Listings: Offers employment clearinghouse.

National Association of Environmental Professionals
389 Main St., Suite 102
Malden, MA 02148
naep.org
Members/Purpose: Persons whose occupations are either directly or indirectly related to environmental management and assessment.
Training: Conducts professional certification program.
Journals/Publications: *Environmental Practice*; *National eNews*
Job Listings: Offers résumé posting service.

National Association of Manufacturers
1331 Pennsylvania Ave. NW
Washington, DC 20004
nam.org
Members/Purpose: Manufacturers; represents industry's views on national and international problems to government.
Journals/Publications: *Briefing*; bulletin; directory of officers, directors, and committees; *Leadership for Manufacturers* magazine; newsletters including *Capital Briefing* and *Just in Time*
Job Listings: None

National Newspaper Association
P.O. Box 7540
Columbus, MO 65205
nna.org
Members/Purpose: Representatives of weekly, semiweekly, and daily newspapers.
Training: None
Journal/Publication: *Publisher's Auxiliary*
Job Listings: None

National Sporting Goods Association

1601 Feehanville Dr.

Mt. Prospect, IL 60056

nsga.org

Members/Purpose: Retailers, manufacturers, wholesalers, and importers of athletic equipment and sporting goods and supplies.

Training: None

Journals/Publications: *NSGA Retail Focus*; *NSGA Sporting Goods Buying Guide*; new products directory; newsletters

Job Listings: None

Public Relations Society of America

33 Maiden Ln.

New York, NY 10038

prsa.org

Members/Purpose: Professional society of public relations practitioners.

Training: Offers professional development programs.

Journals/Publications: *The Strategist*; *Public Relations Tactics*; *Professional Development Guide*; member directory

Job Listings: Job listings posted online; résumés posted online.

Retail Council of Canada

1255 Bay St.

Toronto, ON M5R 2A9

retailcouncil.org

Members/Purpose: Operates as a nonprofit association representing more than 40,000 retail stores including independent merchants, regional and national mass and specialty chains, and online merchants; acts as an advocate of the retail industry.

Training: Sponsors the Canadian Retail Institute and other training and certification opportunities.

Journals/Publications: *Canadian Retailer*; *RCC e-Newsletter*

Job Listings: None

Software & Information Industry Association

1090 Vermont Ave. NW

Washington, DC 20005

siia.net

Members/Purpose: Software vendors, software manufacturers, and other firms involved in the software industry.

Training: None
Journals/Publications: *Upgrade* magazine; e-newsletters
Job Listings: None

Telecommunications Industry Association
2500 Wilson Blvd.
Arlington, VA 22201
tiaonline.org
Members/Purpose: Companies that manufacture products for or provide services to the telecommunications industry.
Training: Sponsors seminars.
Journals/Publications: Newsletters including *TIA Week* and *TIA's Pulse Online*; reports and directories
Job Listings: None

10

Path 5: Teaching

Have you thought much about the possibility of pursuing a teaching career? Teaching is certainly an attractive and rewarding profession and perhaps the most familiar career path of those wanting to directly use their history education. It may even be that a particular teacher was the inspiration for the choice of your history major in college. To work with a body of information you love, and share that enjoyment with countless students over the years, is challenging, enriching, and educational for the instructor, as well as for the student.

Most teachers readily admit they enjoy being students, and good teachers come to the classroom as ready to learn from their students as students arrive hoping to learn from their teachers. Good teachers maintain a regular program of professional development, continuing to learn new classroom techniques, improve their teaching methods, and add to their body of knowledge.

In any academic institution, a fellowship and camaraderie exist among teachers. They share anecdotes about techniques that have or have not worked in the classroom, and many can also share an interest in the growth and development of particular students they have interacted with through the years. Students often come back and visit their formative teachers, and that brings its own rewards.

Talk to history teachers and they'll tell you a surprising fact about their profession. They don't teach history, they teach students. The art of teaching and the skills required in handling the dynamics of student interaction are as important as knowledge of the course content. A college history classroom is populated by considerable numbers of students majoring in history. A teacher's presentation of course material will weigh heavily in the decision process of those students considering continuing their studies in the major. But these history classrooms also have many nonmajors who are taking the course as a general-education requirement or for a minor. These students represent different ages, cultural backgrounds, biases, and issues, and they take their seats in the class with dramatically different degrees of interest in the subject and the teacher. With all that in the way, simply loving history is not enough, though that is certainly important and desirable. How could you begin to teach something you didn't truly enjoy and expect not to convey that disinterest through a mechanical approach to the subject?

Teaching something is an entirely different art from knowing something and demands additional skills. It has very little to do with your own proficiency in the subject. The world is full of extremely skillful practitioners who, for one reason or another and quite often inexplicably, cannot teach someone how they do it. The practice of something is very different from professing it in a classroom.

For example, planning for learning outcomes is critical. Teaching history within an established curriculum means corresponding to some departmental goals and course outlines. Unless you've designed the course, there will be a written course description. To accomplish this body of learning within a set time period requires judicious planning of the material. What will be done each day? How much time to allow between assignments, readings, and labs? What materials to require and what to only recommend? Scores of decisions must be made about how material will be introduced, presented, and ultimately delivered back to you for evaluation.

Add to this the fact that students learn in different ways; some are auditory learners who enjoy listening and gain most of their information in this way. If they are required to take notes *and* listen, something may have to give and it may be difficult for them to retain the material. For others, auditory learning is less successful, and they prefer a visual approach with board work, videos, handouts, their own notes, diagrams, books, and many visual materials. They retain these images and can call them up to remember the material.

Others learn best through reading in class, role plays, team projects, field trips, and other activities that physically involve them. These are kinesthetic learners, and they are often forgotten in planning and curriculum design. The professional teacher ensures that his or her class is satisfying the learning styles of all the students through judicious combinations of modalities in teaching. The professional teacher has analyzed his or her own teaching style and seeks to incorporate those other elements that come less naturally, to ensure all students are reached.

The teaching and learning that take place in a class are not static. The classroom is an emotionally charged environment for the student and instructor that may call into play questions of self-esteem and competency. People are exploring new definitions of themselves in relation to their capabilities, values, or achievement. A good teacher understands this and encourages a risk-free environment of mutual appreciation and participation. Both teacher and student are allowed to make mistakes and move on. The teacher strives to assist in establishing congruence between the self (who we know we are right now), the ideal self (who we want to be), and the learning environment being created in the classroom. Hopefully, the classroom will be a place where the student can rise up and begin to touch his or her ideal self.

Any mention of competency, self-esteem, or self-worth naturally suggests the subject of grading and the evaluations teachers provide. Grades are an expected and required part of many institutional academic settings. Establishing fair and consistent standards of evaluating your students and assigning grades is a significant challenge to many teachers who otherwise feel perfectly competent in the teaching role. Students, too, often complain about grading practices in teachers they, in every other respect, feel positively about.

The teacher of history is called upon to play other roles, too. Animating the class and inspiring attention and commitment to the material are all required in teaching. Part of this is the teacher's enthusiasm, part is teaching style, and part is effective use of ancillary materials and the ability to relate this material to a student's life. History teachers attempt to convey something of the sweep and drama of the human experience over time. More than a dry recitation of dates, places, and names, the best history teacher deals with the impact of these personalities and events on humankind. Wise history instructors can use history as an opportunity to present a range of political and cultural diversity and expose their students to varying perspectives. History is the perfect foil by which an instructor can raise relevant questions, prompt dialogues within the class, and develop within students the discipline of self-questioning and critical thinking. History teachers also clarify difficulties or obscurities in the material and draw parallels or find relationships between examples.

For a professional teacher, each class is an opportunity not only to teach the subject, history, but also to teach how to learn. How to question, record information, be selective, and retain information is an ongoing lesson that takes place in every classroom to some degree.

A good teacher, be it of history or any other subject, also uses the class and the material to explain how this material reflects feelings. Teachers will share their own agreement with or support of ideas or emotions in the material under study. Most of all, an instructor will evaluate and by example develop the student's capacity for self-evaluation through careful, caring feedback about both in- and out-of-class work. The instructor's own example of preparation, organization, personal appearance, evaluation standards, student interest, and enthusiasm will remain an example long after the memory of the actual class content may have faded.

Teachers are very frequently cited as important factors in our choice of a career. Very often teachers will remember one or two of their teachers who were strong influences on their decision to teach. Much of that influence was a result of the teacher's presence in the classroom. These teachers served as models of people enjoying what they were doing and doing it skillfully. They were professional and correct yet remained natural and approachable. We could watch and listen to them and think, "Maybe I could do that."

Definition of the Career Path

We'll look at two possible levels of teaching history: secondary school teaching with a bachelor's degree and college teaching, possibly with a master's degree, but more frequently requiring a doctoral degree as the essential credential.

Secondary School Teaching

Following graduation, certified teachers apply for advertised positions in public middle and high schools. Public school teaching positions are well advertised, and all certified teacher graduates are qualified for entry-level history teaching assignments. Actually, in some situations the first-year teacher's lack of experience can be a plus. With school budgets under terrific strain, principals, superintendents, and other hiring officials may be more attracted to a relatively inexperienced teacher who will earn a lower salary than a more experienced, perhaps higher-degreed teacher who must take a larger proportion of salary funds.

The certification for history teachers is a social science certification, and your degree will most probably be a bachelor of science in social science education. Middle/junior and senior high schools offer a number of courses under the rubric of social sciences, and the prospective history teacher will be called upon to have a far broader social science education than simply history. History most often predominates in the high school social science department; however, there can be classes in geography, government, psychology, and cultures. Here's a recent advertisement for two high school history positions:

High School History Teachers. XXX School District will be hiring history teachers for two high schools in the panhandle area. We are seeking smart, experienced, and passionate teachers who want to work in a student-centered environment of respect and trust with high expectations for all members of the community.

Teachers can expect:

- 24:1 student to teacher ratio
- Classrooms equipped with state-of-the-art-technology and a laptop computer for professional use
- Membership in a professional learning community that fosters respect, trust, risk-taking, openness to learning and the sharing of ideas, and continuously improving practice
- Collaboration as a member of a team that often includes guest artists and/or experts from the community in the design of projects, curriculum, and student outcomes
- Ample planning time to support a collaborative teaching and learning environment
- To teach their subject area course, serve as an adviser to 22 students, and teach one elective course or supervise a student club
- To know their students well, develop a strong sense of community in the classroom, and personalize each student's learning experience
- Accountability and support for student performance toward identified standards
- To meet cooperatively with parents on a scheduled basis to share information about their students and the school
- A demanding learning environment that requires staff to be flexible and problem-solvers who manage ambiguity and adversity well
- Dedication to the vision and best practices of Envision Schools, both in the classroom and as a professional learning community

Salary is commensurate with experience and success in the classroom. Work year is 185 days. Bachelor's degree in history and valid state teaching credential required.

Please submit cover letter and résumé or vitae via e-mail to XXX Schools at jobs@XXXschools.org. College or university transcripts and letters of reference will be requested for those granted interviews.

Of course, the social science education degree draws individuals interested in teaching all of these areas, as well. So in any middle school or high school department, teaching preferences are worked out over time and with seniority, and individuals find themselves with teaching loads that meet the curriculum demands and that they, themselves, enjoy teaching.

Is it possible to teach history at the high school level without state certification in social science education and with a bachelor of arts in history? Yes, in fact, some public school districts that have had difficulty securing teachers, because of location or pay scales, have made provisions to grant temporary certification to noncredentialed teachers. This is, however, not very common, especially since implementation of the No Child Left Behind legislation. Some private high schools might consider a noncertified teacher, although they can and increasingly do require teaching preparation that equals or is very close to that which public schools require. In fact, at some private schools, it is not uncommon for a majority of the history teachers to have master's degrees, and numerous large city high schools have attracted Ph.D.s. Read this current job advertisement for a private school job:

Private School Teacher. XXX School is an independent, coeducational secondary school offering a broad curriculum in the liberal arts. Founded in 1937, the school enrolls 1,100 students in grades 9 through 12 from diverse ethnic, racial, religious, and economic backgrounds. The position requires standing/sitting, walking to other parts of campus, and occasional travel.

The history teacher will join a collaborative department that has significantly reworked its core curriculum and electives to emphasize global perspectives and world cultures. The teacher's assignment will be teaching required courses in United States history. Duties will include, in addition to classroom instruction, acting as an academic adviser to a group of students.

Bachelor's degree in history required, with a master's in history or a related field (ethnic studies, sociology, political science, international studies) preferred. Significant course work in U.S. history expected. The candidate must be able to work with students who vary in ability and learning styles, both nurturing and challenging as necessary, and have experience instructing diverse populations of students.

Salary and benefits are competitive.

Applicants should call 703/555-2347 to request an application form or download a form from the XXX School website (www.XXXschool.org) and should submit it with a résumé and cover letter of interest.

A master's degree in history may be helpful in securing a private school teaching position at the high school level, especially if the master's degree concentration (modern world history, Asian history, and so forth) corresponds to the school's needs.

Teaching with a Master's Degree

Those graduates with master's degrees and no certification at the bachelor's level may also find employment in junior and community college settings or special college programs for adult learners. These schools may welcome the teacher with a master's degree, especially if the specialty is one that corresponds to their curriculum. The following is an advertisement for a college-level history instructor with a master's degree:

History Instructor, XXX County Community College. XXX Community College seeks a professional to teach courses in history, including, but not limited to: world history, age of revolutions, and medieval and renaissance Europe. The individual in this key role will also handle a wide range of professional responsibilities and activities from attending department and college meetings and participating on committees to advising students and handling other duties as assigned. This position may require teaching on load at on- and off-campus sites, both day and evening schedules. This is a full-time, entry-level, tenure-track position.

Requires a master's degree in history with concentrations in world and/or European history. A background teaching at the community college level and bilingual skills preferred.

Please send cover letter, résumé and the name, address and telephone number of three (3) business references by June 1 to . . .

Similar positions, even those requiring a high level of specialization, can be found in community colleges and some four-year schools. A rewarding teaching career in history at the college level with a master's degree, is possible. Two-year and community college work can provide a long and productive career within the same institution or provide the opportunity for a lateral move to a similar type of school. At the same time, however, it is important to caution you that if you are interested in moving from that type of institution to a four-year college or university, it may be difficult without an advanced degree, despite the fact that you may have years of teaching experience.

There are also some jobs teaching at the four-year college level with a master's degree in history. Nevertheless, the movement, expectation, and market demand would be for the doctoral degree, and it is that degree that will provide the most security of both employment and employment opportunities for a teaching career at the college and university level in history.

Teaching with a Doctoral Degree

The doctoral degree in history opens up the world of college teaching to the prospective educator. Competition here is keen, but positions are well-advertised in vehicles such as *The Chronicle of Higher Education* (chronicle.com), a weekly publication reporting on higher education issues and containing the most complete listing of faculty, staff, and leadership position openings for colleges and universities in the United States and some foreign countries. The following is an ad for a position at a Canadian institution that would be of interest to a new Ph.D. in history.

History Instructor. The Department of History invites applications for a history instructor position with a one-year term. The position will involve teaching both history majors and those meeting general education requirements. Candidates should have relevant postsecondary teaching experience. Minimum qualification for this term position is an M.A. in history. Preference will be given to candidates with a Ph.D. (those with all but dissertation completed welcome to apply) and a specialization in pre- and post-Confederation Canada. The teaching load would consist of 4 classes per semester.

An application must include: curriculum vitae, copies of transcripts, copies of course outlines, copies of teaching evaluations, samples of research/publications, and a list of at least three referees. Information about salary and benefits is available from the college's website.

This advertisement indicates that the successful candidate will be teaching both required and general education history classes. Teaching core curriculum history courses is generally part of the teaching load of new college faculty. Many of the students will be taking history classes because it is a college requirement for graduation and not because they are history majors or have chosen the course. The history or social science department performs a service to the entire college in offering this course. Generally, even senior faculty will teach at least one offering of a lower-level survey of history, though as you become more senior in the faculty you can take on courses that are more directly related to your interests and educational background.

Applicants responding to this advertisement should be ready to document their teaching success. This could come from teaching assistantships done while working on the doctoral degree. Many students acquire this experience as graduate teaching assistants, part-time faculty, lecturers, or adjunct faculty at other colleges or programs. The advertisement also calls for a specialization in pre- and post-Confederation Canada. This could be demonstrated either through transcript submission showing course work in that area, published articles or papers on some aspect of those issues, or recommendations from colleagues on your expertise in those areas.

For many college and university teaching positions, a doctorate is not only preferred, but required. Keep in mind that the road to a doctorate is fairly long and arduous. Along the way, you'll meet some wonderful people, some who'll be friends and colleagues the rest of your life. Even colleagues separated by long distances have the opportunity to revisit at conferences and symposia. You'll have opportunities to write, teach, and perhaps publish—all before you finish your degree. Take advantage of these opportunities when you can. As the advertisement in this section suggests, some of those kinds of qualifications will be asked of you. However, it is possible to become overly involved in some of these areas to the detriment of degree progress.

Working Conditions

The working conditions for teachers of history are dramatically different according to the educational setting.

Secondary School Classrooms

The high school history teacher has a full complement of classes, perhaps as many as five or six a day, and may have study hall or lunchroom supervision duties during the week, responsibilities for some after-school detention centers, or even a sports activity to supervise. The place of discipline in the secondary curriculum has a major impact in the classroom and is perhaps the single most dominant element of the working conditions for the secondary history teacher. Since the student population is not voluntary, resistance is prevalent and acting out through poor discipline and bad behavior is common.

The effective classroom teacher is one who has successfully mastered classroom management. For many young teachers, these are the most challenging lessons and make for the most interesting stories as they grow in their profession. An equal balance between teaching history and classroom discipline seldom exists and can be particularly frustrating, as when one disruptive student threatens the order of an otherwise studious class.

Most public high schools are fairly rigid systems of enforced behavior norms, and the principal agents of that enforcement are the faculty. To elect high school history education as your particular arena is to challenge your ability to maintain your poise, focus on your subject matter, and interest in training and shaping young people, while at the same time requiring you to both enforce and administer the necessary disciplinary elements mandated by your school. These sanctions include grades, dismissal, detention, warnings, parent conferences, and referrals to other helping agencies in or out of the school system.

Teaching in a high school entails a full day with fairly rigid starting and ending times and much at-home work. Some of the busiest of those at-home schedules belong to the history faculty. History curriculums in middle school and high school often emphasize content mastery, so evaluative instruments such as quizzes and examinations are frequently employed to provide feedback to both the instructor and students on their grasp of the material. Grading these exams, quizzes, and essays and providing that all-important feedback is a take-home assignment night after night. Staying ahead of text and book assignments is also time consuming, as is maintaining required records of attendance, grades, warnings, progress reports, and other documentation that may be required in your school district.

High school history teachers often take on other assignments such as homeroom duty, field trips, guest speakers, chaperoning duties, and advising activities for yearbooks, literary journals, or clubs in the school. These also can be very time demanding, and it is important that the teacher entering into secondary history teaching understands that these assignments are not so much additions but typically part of what makes up a high school teaching professional's commitment.

College Classrooms

A college teaching environment is significantly different from a middle or high school setting. There is less need to appease a number of outside publics. Teachers do not need to satisfy school boards or parent-teacher groups. The world of the college classroom is closed to outsiders and isn't violated by anyone outside the class. This is such an accepted convention that it is, in fact, rare to have a class interrupted by anyone outside of the room. Academic freedom protects professors in large part, allowing them to express themselves within their class material with far greater pointedness than in a high school class.

Grading, evaluation procedures, the number of tests, and even the issue of whether to have textbooks or texts may be entirely up to the faculty member, and if the rationale supports these decisions the university will seldom interfere. An added protection is the granting of tenure to established professors who have documented significant teaching histories and excellent student evaluations, publications, campus committee work, and outreach to the community. The granting of tenure gains teaching staff an additional degree of job security and further supports their expression of academic freedom. All of these conditions make the classroom environment and the relations of faculty and students very different from what has come before in the student's education.

The actual teaching day in a college or university setting involves fewer class hours taught per day and per week. At an institution that focuses on faculty research, the teacher would be responsible for teaching two to three courses that each meets three to four hours per week. Schools that emphasize teaching rather than research require instructors to teach three to four courses for a total of nine to twelve hours of class meetings per week. These class hours and some mandated office hours for advising class students and general advisees are the principal requirements for attendance on the faculty member's part. But as the next ad makes clear, there are other expectations.

History, two positions, XXX University. An earned doctorate, ABD considered, in early modern Europe and U.S. history since the Civil War with teaching experience in higher education preferred. Teaching responsibilities include teaching both world history surveys and upper division courses in area(s) of specialization. Position is tenure track with salary and rank based upon the candidate's qualifications. Candidates must demonstrate a vital Christian faith and integrate the Christian faith with teaching and learning within the tenets of the Baptist faith and message. Position will begin August 15. Applicants should send a letter of application, curriculum vitae, unofficial transcripts, and the names and addresses of three references to ffairs@XXXcollege.edu.

In addition to courses and advising, scholarly research is an expectation even at those colleges where tenure is not based on publication. All colleges want their faculty to contribute to the scholarly dialogue in their discipline, and this is reviewed by chairs of departments and academic deans periodically throughout the instructor's career. It may be a determining element in granting tenure or promotion to that faculty member and may influence issues such as salary negotiations, merit increases, and the like.

Committee work is also important, as the faculty at most colleges are the governing and rule-making bodies who determine and vote on governance and program changes. Committee work can be issue-oriented, such as a commission on the status of women or a faculty pay equity survey. It may be programmatic, such as a committee to study the core curriculum for undergraduates or to devise a new graphic arts major; it may be related to credentials, as in a committee set up to prepare materials for an accreditation visit.

Some committees, such as those on academic standards, curriculum review, promotion and tenure, planning and administrator review committees, are permanent, though the members may change on a rotating schedule. Other groups are formed for a limited time or until completion of some task. These committees are essential and serve as a vehicle for guiding the direction of the school. Having the support of all the faculty and constantly fresh and interested members helps to ensure all voices are heard and many different opinions considered in making what are often long-reaching decisions.

A college day is certainly less rigid than a high school schedule, though it may be just as busy and as long. The difference in content is that for the high-school teacher, much of the day and commitment are enforced and required. The college teacher may certainly feel institutional and professional pressures on fulfilling certain roles, but the actual election of how to do that is up to the individual. There will be classes, office hours, meetings, and research work to do. Since college campuses are often wonderful centers of art, music, and intellectual exchange, there are frequently events to attend in the evening. Faculty members may act as advisers to fraternities, sororities, campus newspapers, and clubs, which may also add to their day.

Training and Qualifications

To teach history at the secondary level requires a bachelor of science degree in social science education at the secondary level and certification for the state or province in which you wish to teach. These programs are well-defined options within the education curriculum or the social science department of many teacher training colleges and universities. They include a teaching practicum where you would have the opportunity to leave campus and teach actual history classes under a supervising teacher for an academic semester or quarter. Certification for the state granting the degree is usually part of the degree process and may include the requirement to participate in the PRAXIS teacher examinations offered through the Educational Testing Service (ets.org). In states requiring these exams, appropriate test preparation is usually well incorporated into the curriculum.

Another option for the individual with a degree in history who desires to teach but lacks certification would be to enroll in a "conversion" program at a college or university. These programs offer an opportunity to add the necessary state-mandated teaching requirements to their existing degree. Depending on your undergraduate degree and whether a change of institution is involved, this could require twelve to eighteen months of academic enrollment and, in some cases, a full two years.

Such conversion programs can also exist independent of a collegiate institution. Some are the product of a consortium of school districts, such as The Upper Valley Teacher Institute (uvti.org) in Lebanon, New Hampshire. This innovative, nonclassroom teacher qualifying program takes bachelor-degreed individuals, many of whom have had other careers or significant work experience, and places them with master teachers in actual classrooms for a full year. Half the year is at one grade level and the remaining half of the year with another grade. The year includes much independent work and follows a contract established at the start of the year. There may be a requirement to participate in an associated classroom program to meet state reading certification requirements, as well.

College and university teaching requires the doctorate or, in some cases, all but the dissertation (sometimes known informally known as ABD) completed. Salary and assignments may be affected by lack of an earned doctorate. In addition to the doctorate, we have seen there may be requirements for teaching experience, special depth of research or practice in a particular genre or subject area in history, and some additional competencies. There is almost always the requirement of teaching basic survey classes to first- and second-year students.

Earnings

Middle and secondary school teachers of history are paid according to the same salary schedules as other teachers in their school district. Salaries across the nation vary depending on location, which affects cost of living and level of support of education as reflected in the school budget. Salary information is easy to find on the Internet. The American Federation of Teachers' website (aft.org) contains the latest teacher salary survey. Look for a table that shows salary information for entry-level positions by state.

At the time this edition was published, teachers' salaries averaged $46,597. Beginning teachers averaged just under $32,000 per year.

According to Education Canada, teachers with a four-year degree averaged between $30,341 and $68,976 yearly in 2004, depending on the province (with highest salaries in Alberta and lowest in Prince Edwards Island).

Average college faculty earnings are affected by type of institution, geographic area, field of study, and faculty rank. The American Association of

University Professors (aaup.org) reported that in 2004–2005, the average faculty salary across all fields and types of institutions was $68,505. Those with the rank of instructor averaged slightly less than $40,000, while those holding the rank of full professor (the highest rank) averaged close to $92,000 annually. Remember, these are average figures for all college faculty. As a professor in history, your earnings may be lower because of job market factors, if you teach at a private school or small institution, or if you teach at a two-year college.

Career Outlook

Projected career outlooks vary depending on the level of education at which you would like to teach. Be sure to review the following information very carefully and be ready to implement a job search strategy that takes the current job market into account.

Secondary School Teaching

The U.S. Department of Labor, Bureau of Labor Statistics, reports that employment of secondary school teachers is expected to grow about as fast as the average for all occupations through the year 2014. Signing bonuses, loans for moving expenses, and loan-forgiveness programs are some of the enticements being used to attract qualified candidates, at least in some areas.

Higher Education

The Bureau of Labor Statistics reports that employment of college faculty is expected to increase much faster than the average for all occupations through 2014. As you consider employment in academe, though, one important trend worth researching is the increasing use of part-time faculty. Almost 50 percent of the professoriate are now employed part-time. There are many reasons for this large number, but the bottom line is that there is heavy competition for full-time, tenure-track positions in higher education.

Other factors worth investigating are current trends in the use of tenure, population trends, and the resulting number of students expected to attend college; whether a minimum faculty retirement age is currently required; and the number of individuals currently pursuing advanced degrees in history. *The Chronicle of Higher Education* (chronicle.com), the American Association of University Professors (aaup.org), and the Canadian Association of University Teachers (caut.ca) can provide up-to-date information.

Strategies for Finding the Jobs

Depending on your level of education, the grade level you hope to teach, and the type of school where you would like to work, your strategy for finding the history teaching job will vary. We have outlined efforts to undertake if you are interested in teaching in a public school, in a private school, or in an institution of higher education. Each requires its own strategy, so review the section that pertains to your interests.

The Public Schools
A number of simple measures can lead to identifying teaching positions.

- **Scan relevant newspaper ads.** The public school teacher candidate is advised to make a regular practice of scanning newspaper advertisements. The Internet allows you to scan listings from all over the country. In addition, the public library often has a selection of local papers that you can look through.
- **Check with your career office.** College, university, and technical school career offices in your region of the state will also be on the mailing list to receive teaching vacancy announcements. Determine which schools' job postings you can view through reciprocity agreements with your own college and make these visits part of your regular job search. You will find that you become so practiced at screening newspapers and job postings that it will take very little time to quickly ascertain if any new openings have been listed.
- **Directly contact schools where you'd like to work.** Send a cover letter and résumé to those schools where you would like to work. (Almost all have websites where you can obtain information about employment, and in some cases you can submit applications electronically.) In addition, websites of state and provincial departments of education can provide helpful information about their schools.

The Private Schools
To identify openings in private schools, follow steps similar to those used with public schools, but don't overlook resources that are specific to public schools.

- **Directly contact schools where you'd like to work.** Send a cover letter and résumé to each private school where you'd like to work. In addition to their own websites and local yellow page listings, private schools may be identified through sources such as Peterson's website (petersons.com) or *The Handbook of Private Schools* published by Porter

Sargent. You will find both of these references useful in your job search. Also visit the National Association of Independent Schools' website (nais.org) for information on how to find employment; to review selected articles from their journal, *Independent School;* or to search for schools.

• **Attend job fairs.** Find out about job fairs and attend as many as you can. Job fairs for private schools, in the United States and abroad, are held year-round. Many are administered by recruiting firms. These fairs serve as a major entree for many job seekers into the private school system. You register your materials with a private school placement agency, which then provides access to a private school job fair where you can meet and interact with a number of hiring officials from a regional or national base. Your college career office can put you in touch with some of these private school recruiting firms.

Possible Employers

One advantage of a teaching career is that there are so many potential employers. These include both public and private schools as well as postsecondary institutions.

Public Schools

More than 1.2 million teachers are employed as secondary school teachers in the United States and Canada. Geographic employment distribution matches that of the general population. School districts are vying for the best candidates, so positions are well advertised. Use the strategy suggestions shown in the previous section to identify positions in which you are interested.

Department of Defense (DOD) Schools

Since 1946 there have been schools on U.S. military bases around the world for children of military and civilian personnel assigned overseas. Just under three hundred schools serve this segment of U.S. public education, and courses of study, eligibility for teachers, textbooks, and programs parallel those of the public schools in the United States. Schools in the DOD system are all accredited by the North Central Association of Colleges and Schools. The U.S. Department of Defense Education Activity website (odedodea.edu) contains all the information you will need to decide whether you want to pursue this teaching option. Employment listings are shown, and application information and forms are available for downloading.

Private Schools in the United States and Canada

According to About.com, there are 30,400 schools enrolling more than 6.4 million students in the United States. The National Association of Independent Schools (nais.org) reports that approximately 25 percent of all schools are private. More than 1,700 private schools serve Canadian students. Accessing the private school market is a very different process from seeking a public school situation. In general, there is not a significant amount of "crossover" between the two systems, public and private, and teachers within the private school system tend to stay within that educational environment.

Private schools list positions and send out job notices but seldom advertise in newspapers to ensure a more select pool of candidates and to maintain a lower profile than their public school counterparts. As tuition-driven institutions, they do not have the core franchise market that public schools have and must seek students through reputation and discreet advertising.

Private Schools Abroad

The Internal Educator (TIE) has a website (tieonline.com) where you can subscribe to the *International Educator* job openings list. Also review the *ISS Directory of International Schools*, published by International Schools Services.

Resources for Finding Both Public and Private School Openings

Educational Directories, a major publisher of educational resources (ediusa.com), produces *Patterson's Elementary Education* and *Patterson's American Education* each year. They list public and private elementary and secondary schools, school districts and superintendents, postsecondary schools, and others, including nursery schools, YMCA programs, and the like. Use these directories to conduct your proactive job search activities: mailing out cover letters and résumés, networking, and conducting telephone follow-up. You can check out Canadian information at Canadian Teachers.net (http://canada.teachers.net).

Career offices, online job sites, and organizations related to education or employment often carry job vacancy listings that include teaching positions. The American Association for Employment in Education's website (aaee.org) lists job vacancies and job search resources, as does Job Canada (jobcanada.org).

In addition, be sure to carefully review the list of professional associations for teachers of history, which follows this section. For several associations there is a line labeled "Job Listings," and any activities that the association undertakes to assist its members in finding employment are shown.

College and University Jobs

Acquiring a college teaching position nearly always demands that you relocate to an institution other than where you received your degree. Higher education has limited openings at any one time, and part-time work or adjunct faculty status at one institution is no guarantee of earning a full-time spot. Most departments have budget lines dedicated to potentially full-time, tenured faculty. That means that faculty who are hired in those budget lines are hired with the expectation they will become a permanent part of the faculty and earn tenure and promotion when they qualify.

Consequently, though there may be schools you would enjoy teaching at or areas of the country you would prefer, the supply and demand of college professorships clearly dictate that you must follow the demand and relocate.

Go to "The Source." *The Chronicle of Higher Education* (chronicle.com) lists two-year college, four-year college, and university teaching positions in history in the United States, Canada, and some other countries. If you don't have convenient access to a hard copy or the online version, your career center, department office, and college library will all have copies you can review each week.

Network with Faculty Colleagues. Another excellent source of information about college-level positions will be your own faculty colleague contacts made as you pursue your advanced degree. There is a well-established network that becomes very active when schools are seeking to fill a position and would enjoy the personal recommendation of a friend or former teaching associate to do the very best by the hiring institution. For this reason, it's important to ensure that your faculty mentors and colleagues are well aware of your teaching and research interests and geographic preferences so they can respond for you and move the process along if an opportunity presents itself.

Attend Professional Meetings. Interviews are often conducted at professional meetings where recent job openings may be announced or posted in a conspicuous place at the registration table. As a graduate student, many of these conferences are available to you at substantially reduced fees or no fee at all, and you should take advantage of them for the professional content and the opportunity to meet representatives from the departments of other higher education institutions.

Possible Job Titles

For the professional educator, there is not a wide latitude in job title. The term *teacher* is so old and so esteemed that we use it to apply to professionals from nursery school to the most rarefied levels of postdoctoral research. All are teachers. We see variants from time to time; for example, the resource room teacher in elementary school who works individually with students experiencing difficulties in particular subjects or the skills application teacher on the college faculty who may have a more narrowly defined teaching role than a staff professor. To students, however, these distinctions may not loom very large and most are made to indicate bureaucratic distinctions. The teaching role remains the same.

Assistant professor of history
Associate professor of history
Cooperating teacher
Educator
History instructor
History lecturer
History teacher
Instructor in history and social sciences
Professor of history
Social science teacher
Teacher

Related Occupations

Teaching skills and teacher training lend themselves to innumerable occupations and are seen as universally valuable by all other employers. The ability to explain, demonstrate, encourage, and test and spark the imagination can be transferred to countless settings in business and industry. The introduction of new products, cross-training of staff, planning for change or transition, or responding to crises are all situations that call for a teacher's expertise.

Public museums, cultural programs for children, national parks, and public relations organizations all have need of the teacher's training in presentation skills, explanation, and the ability to convey meaning.

Social service programs devote much of their mission to education in the form of new programs and information for their clients that would use teachers in situations not very different from the standard classroom. The following list is a very brief and very general suggestion of the possible related careers for the history teacher.

Counselor
Education administrator
Educational consultant

Employee development specialist
Employment interviewer
Environmental educator
Hospital/community health educator
Human resources specialist
Librarian
Media relations representative
Nonprofit organization administrator
Preschool worker
Public relations specialist
Researcher
Sales representative
Social worker
Trainer

Professional Associations for Teachers of History

Finding out about and joining at least one professional association can play an important role in achieving success in your job search. Many associations relate to the kinds of jobs available for teachers of history. Listed here are some groups that can provide valuable information in terms of finding out about actual job listings or talking with members for networking purposes.

American Association of Community Colleges
1 Dupont Circle NW, Suite 410
Washington, DC 20036
aacc.nche.edu
Members/Purpose: Community, technical, and junior colleges; individual associates interested in community college development; corporate, educational, foundation, and international associate members.
Training: Conducts seminars and professional training programs.
Journals/Publications: *AACJC Community College Times*; *Community College Journal*; *AACC Letter*; membership directory; research briefs
Job Listings: None

American Association of State Colleges and Universities
1307 New York Ave. NW
Washington, DC 20005-4701
aascu.org

Members/Purpose: Colleges and universities offering programs leading to a degree of bachelor, master, or doctor that are wholly or partially state supported and controlled.
Training: Conducts national and regional workshops.
Journals/Publications: *Public Purpose*; ad hoc reports; and studies
Job Listings: None

American Association of University Professors
1012 14th St. NW, Suite 500
Washington, DC 20005
aaup.org
Members/Purpose: College and university teachers, research scholars, and academic librarians; purposes are to facilitate cooperation among teachers and research scholars in universities, colleges, and professional schools, for the promotion of higher education and research, and to increase the usefulness and advance the standards, ideals, and welfare of the profession.
Training: None
Journals/Publications: *Academe*; guidebooks, newsletters, and brochures
Job Listings: None

American Federation of Teachers
555 New Jersey Ave. NW
Washington, DC 20001
aft.org
Members/Purpose: AFL-CIO; works with teachers and other educational employees at the state and local level in organizing, collective bargaining, research, educational issues, and public relations; conducts research in various areas.
Training: None
Journals/Publications: *American Academic*; *American Educator*; *American Teacher*; *Healthwire*; *AFT on Campus*; *PSRP Reporter*
Job Listings: None

American Historical Association
400 A St. SE
Washington, DC 20003
historians.org
Members/Purpose: Professional historians, educators, and others interested in promoting historical studies and collecting and preserving historical manuscripts.

Training: None
Journals/Publications: *Perspectives*; *American Historical Review*; *Directory of Historical Departments and Organizations in the United States and Canada*; directories and other publications
Job Listings: See newsletter.

Canadian Association of University Teachers
2705 Queensview Dr.
Ottawa, ON K2B 8K2
caut.ca
Members/Purpose: Represents some 55,000 Canadian teachers, librarians, researchers, and other academic professionals and general staff; works to improve the quality and accessibility of postsecondary education.
Training: Offers educational programs, primarily at member associations' location.
Journals/Publications: *CAUT Bulletin*; *CAUT Almanac of Post-Secondary Education*; legal reviews, briefs, and reports
Job Listings: None

(Canadian) Society for the Advancement of Excellence in Education
225-1889 Springfield Rd.
Kelowna, BC V1Y 5V5
saee.bc.ca
Members/Purpose: Provides nonpartisan education research and information to policy makers, education partners, and the public. Encourages higher performance throughout Canada's public education system.
Training: Hosts workshops, seminars, and symposia.
Journals/Publications: *Education Analyst*; research reports on Canadian education
Job Listings: List of job openings on website.

Canadian Teachers' Federation
2490 Don Reid Ave.
Ottawa, ON K1H 1E
ctf-fce.ca
Members/Purpose: Operates as a national federation of 16 member organizations and an affiliate member representing more than 215,000 teachers across Canada; serves as an advocate for the teaching profession and a strong public education system.

Training: None
Journals/Publications: *Horizon Magazine*; *PD Perspectives*
Job Listings: None

National Association of Independent Schools
1620 L St. NW
Washington, DC 20036
nais.org
Members/Purpose: Independent elementary and secondary school members; regional associations of independent schools and related associations; provides curricular and administrative research and services.
Training: Conducts seminars.
Journals/Publications: *Independent School*; NAIS e-Bulletin
Job Listings: General teacher's packet that consists of recruitment agencies, placement firms, directories, and brochures that help with choosing the right school.

National Educational Association
1201 16th St. NW
Washington, DC 20036
nea.org
Members/Purpose: Professional organization and union of elementary and secondary school teachers, college and university professors, administrators, principals, counselors, and others concerned with education.
Training: None
Journals/Publications: *NEA Today*; *Higher Education Advocate*; *Tomorrow's Teachers*; *Education Statistics*
Job Listings: None

Organization of American Historians
112 N. Bryan St.
Bloomington, IN 47408
oah.org
Members/Purpose: Professional historians, including college faculty members, secondary school teachers, graduate students, and other individuals in related fields; institutional subscribers are college, university, high school, and public libraries, and historical agencies.
Training: None
Journals/Publications: *Journal of American History*, *OAH Magazine of History*, newsletter
Job Listings: None

Index